# The Whispers Of Wenatchee

## A Collection of Natural Expression

### Volume II

**Written by**

The Breathers of Wenatchee Air

**Edited & Curated by**

C.G. Dahlin

Emmi Bartholdt

**Translations by**

Anabel Watson

# Contributing Writers (68):

*Returning Contributor = ***

Adam Leonardini (1)*
Allyssa Arnold (7)
Anabel Watson (6)*
Anna Marie Sullivan (5)
Ben Anon (1)
Betsy Dudash (4)
Buddy Pierce (3)
Cameron Curtis (3)
C.G. Dahlin (5)
Chad Ruggles (2)
Charles K. Chuckenspire (4)
Christine Ingram (1)*
Cougar Penhaligon (2)*
Dalilia Villamil (4)*
Diana Rigelman (4)
Diana Romero (1)
Donovon Griggs (1)
Doug Copenspire (1)
Eric W. Fotherby (5)*
Eric J. Stepper (4)
Ethan Starkey (1)
Faith Merz (4)
Gary Trader (1)
Gavin Johnson (2)
Gloria Piper Roberson (8)*
Greg Wright (1)
Holly Thorpe (2)
Ian Ford (4)
Jana Divis (3)
Jazmyn Jira (3)
Jesemynn Cacka (7)*
Jon Davies (5)
Judie Peavey (4)
Katharine Kiendl (2)*
Kendra Barahona (3)
Kennedy Clark (2)
Kevin Lane Strickland (3)*
Kristina Stepper (2)
L. Burton Brender (7)*
Linda Reid (5)
Linnea Charmaine Rigelman (1)
Lorna Osborne (1)
Martha Flores (3)
Matthew Genther (2)*
Matthew "Suihei" Morgan (7)

Maximus Ceballos (2)*
Michael Reed Schooler (4)*
Mike Morgan (3)*
Moon Rae (2)
Mitch McCarrell (5)*
Noah Massey (2)
Pat Turner (1)
Rachel Beardslee (1)
Ray Sharp (4)
Ruth Joy (2)
Russell Babbitt (4)
Ryan Ochoa (3)
Sabrina B (3)
Sylvia B (9)*
T.J. Rodriguez (3)
Taylor Lisa Bailey (1)
Tony Yetter (1)
Tyler Burlingame (2)*
Ulises Navarro (6)*
Vic Tapscott (2)
Wendy Howard (2)
Zoe Zamorano (3)*

# Table Of Contents

## I

The Inward by Michael Reed Schooler ...................... pg. 2
Failure by Mitch McCarrell ..................................... pg. 3
Kill by Jesemynn Cacka .......................................... pg. 4
Letter To The Editor by Russell Babbitt .................. pg. 5
The Difference Between Poems... by Judie Peavey .... pg. 6
Peace I Ask Of Thee, Oh River by Linda Reid ........... pg. 6
The Wasting Poet by Kevin Lane Strickland ............. pg. 7
09/12/19 by Jon Davies ....................................... pg. 10
Mid by Ulises Navarro .......................................... pg. 10
Selfishness In Print by Jon Davies ....................... pg. 11

## II

Motherhood by Taylor Lisa Bailey .......................... pg. 13
2:15 A.M. by Faith Merz ....................................... pg. 14
The Woman by Gloria Piper Roberson .................... pg. 15
A Day With The Facundo... by Ulises Navarro ......... pg. 19
Sunoco Row by Eric W. Fotherby ........................... pg. 20
The Northwest Passage by L. Burton Brender ......... pg. 23
People by Eric J. Stepper ..................................... pg. 24
How Are You by Cougar Penhaligon ...................... pg. 25

## III

Wenatchee Driving Test by Mike Morgan ................ pg. 27
Wrecked by Maximus Cellabos ............................. pg. 31
March 12th, 2012 by Diana Romero ...................... pg. 32
Untitled by Donovan Griggs .................................. pg. 33
The Wenatchee Curse by C.G. Dahlin ..................... pg. 35
Homestead Bones by Gloria Piper Roberson ........... pg. 36
Coming Home by Buddy Pierce ............................. pg. 37
These Are The Days by Betsy Dudash .................... pg. 39
Home by Diana Rigelman ..................................... pg. 39
Joyful Mornings by Eric W. Fotherby ..................... pg. 40
Rabbit Humps by Buddy Pierce ............................. pg. 42
Aubade 206 by Mitch McCarrell ............................ pg. 44
Quaint by L. Burton Brender ................................ pg. 45
To Be On The Radar by Jana Divis ....................... pg. 46

# IV

Tops Down, Bottom's Up by Michael Reed Schooler.. pg.48
I Do Not Consent by Russell Babbitt ...................... pg. 49
Exit Us by Greg Wright ........................................... pg. 50
Sandcastles by Matthew "Suihei" Morgan .............. pg. 53
Sanitary Insanity by Matthew "Suihei" Morgan ....... pg. 53
Mirage by Matthew "Suihei" Morgan ...................... pg. 53
Stepping Outside Pattern by Allyssa Arnold .......... pg. 53
Terrorism Within The... by Eric W. Fotherby .......... pg. 54
The Day The Music Died by Russell Babbitt .......... pg. 56
Capitalism On An Airplane by Anabel Watson ........ pg. 59
Home Buyer by L. Burton Brender ....................... pg. 59
Ignore-ance by Matthew "Suihei" Morgan ............... pg. 59
What The Tortoise Taught Me by Sylvia B ............. pg. 60
Clever Disguise by Allyssa Arnold ......................... pg. 61
Heart Smart by Kristina Stepper .......................... pg. 61
Mama Says by Matthew Genther .......................... pg. 62
Kali by Katharine Kiendl ..................................... pg. 63

# V

Whirled by Tony Yetter ........................................ pg. 65
Sink Me Into The Earth by Anabel Watson ............. pg. 69
Thresholds by Linda Reid ..................................... pg. 70
Palos Verdes Blue by Gavin Johnson ..................... pg. 70
Man On The Moon by Faith Merz .......................... pg. 71
Moonpearl by Ray Sharp ...................................... pg. 71
The One Who Walks by C.G. Dahlin ...................... pg. 72
Rain by Sylvia B .................................................. pg. 73
Poem-kus* by Eric J. Stepper................................ pg. 74
Listen by Faith Merz ............................................ pg. 74
The Mother's Song by C.G. Dahlin ........................ pg. 75
The Moon And The Star by Wendy Howard ............ pg. 76
Ice Tear by Kendra Barahona ............................... pg. 78
Fate, A Waiting Game by Anabel Watson ................ pg. 78
Early One Winter... by Gloria Piper Roberson ......... pg. 78
Little Ghosts by Lorna Osborne ............................ pg. 79
Untitled by Vic Tapscott ...................................... pg. 79
To See Again by Ulises Navarro ............................ pg. 80
Miraculous Disentropy by Ray Sharp ..................... pg. 80
His Grace by Gloria Piper Roberson ...................... pg. 81
Blue Planet by Delilah Villamil .............................. pg. 81
Mother (Nature), Can You Hear... by Sylvia B ......... pg. 82

# VI

Double Body by Delilah Villamil ............................ pg. 84
Always + Never by Matthew Genther ..................... pg. 84
The Twisted Stems Of...by Kevin Lane Strickland ... pg. 85
Moonlit Saunter by Allyssa Arnold ........................ pg. 86
Sunday, March 6th... by Cougar Penhaligon .......... pg. 87
Mystical Path by Allyssa Arnold ............................ pg. 91
The Thought by Delilah Villamil ............................ pg. 91
Shadow Work by Charles K. Chuckenspire ............. pg. 92
The Ghost Called Solitude by Martha Flores .......... pg. 93
Space Is An Eye Inside of... by Chad Ruggles ........ pg. 93
Language of One by Jazmyn Jira ......................... pg. 94
The Human Brain by Delilah Villamil ..................... pg. 95
Sacred Home by Allyssa Arnold ............................ pg. 95
Yearnings by Zoe Zamorano ................................. pg. 96
Complicated by Linda Reid .................................... pg. 96
Roles We Play by Allyssa Arnold ........................... pg. 96
Emotions by Anabel Watson .................................. pg. 97
Untitled by Cameron Curtis .................................. pg. 97
Mixed Bag by Charles K. Chuckenspire ................. pg. 98

# VII

The Thing by Jesemynn Cacka ............................ pg. 101
Kindergarten by L. Burton Brender ...................... pg. 102
Famous As Fuck by Mitch McCarrell ..................... pg. 103
Untitled by Tyler Burlingame ............................... pg. 104
Sunshine And Rainbows by Kendra Barahona ...... pg. 104
Picky Eater by Kennedy Clark .............................. pg. 105
Fall by L. Burton Brender .................................... pg. 105
Broken Halos by Sylvia B .................................... pg. 106
The Hearts Of Children by Pat Turner .................. pg. 107
Children In Cages by Martha Flores ..................... pg. 109
Bosnian Child by Gloria Piper Roberson .............. pg. 109
Treasures Of A Grandma's Heart by Linda Reid .... pg. 110
Cashmere Childhood... by Doug Copenspire.......... pg. 110
Picking Out A Walking... by Rachel Beardslee ....... pg. 111
The Pit by Buddy Pierce ..................................... pg. 113
Letter To A Parent Taken By...by Jazmyn Jira ...... pg. 115
Children by Eric J. Stepper .................................. pg. 116

# VIII

Moribund by Ulises Navarro ............................... pg. 118
Blood by Eric W. Fotherby ........................... pg. 118
Reincarnation by Anna Marie Sullivan ................. pg. 119
Black And White... by Gloria Piper Roberson ........ pg. 120
Scrambled by Jesemynn Cacka .......................... pg. 121
Rag by Ulises Navarro .......................................... pg. 121
Old Dirt Road by L. Burton Brender .................... pg. 122
Untitled by Christine Ingram ............................ pg. 122
Mundane Nothingness by Zoe Zamorano ............. pg. 123
Untitled by Cameron Curtis ............................... pg. 125
Plans We Make by Judie Peavey .......................... pg. 126
The Night Before My... by L. Burton Brender ........ pg. 127
Seth, U.S. Army... by Gloria Piper Roberson ........ pg. 128
11 A.M. by Noah Massey ................................... pg. 128
Street Of Broken Dreams by Judie Peavey ........... pg. 129
The Psych Ward In My Head by Ian Ford ............. pg. 129
A Snapshot From ... by Gloria Piper Roberson ...... pg. 129
Three Little Words by Diana Rigelman ................ pg. 130
Untitled by Ruth Joy ........................................ pg. 133
Skin by Sylvia B ............................................... pg. 135
Blood by Holly Thorpe ....................................... pg. 136
Wicked Hunt by Cameron Curtis ....................... pg. 137
Desperately... by Matthew "Suihei" Morgan ......... pg. 137
Lost In The... by Matthew "Suihei" Morgan .......... pg. 138
Carnage by Anna Marie Sullivan ........................ pg. 138
Robert Stapler's Letter by Noah Massey .............. pg. 139
Words Under Surveillance by Ian Ford ................. pg. 142
Addiction by T.J. Rodriguez ............................... pg. 142
Sweet Sylvia by Sylvia B .................................... pg. 143
Midwife of Death by Jesemynn Cacka ................. pg. 144
Farewell Again by Mike Morgan ......................... pg. 145
A Portrait Of Courage by Linda Reid .................. pg. 149
The Dreamer... by Matthew "Suihei" Morgan ........ pg. 150
Grief by Katharine Kiendl ................................. pg. 150
Countering Suicide by Ian Ford .......................... pg. 151
Moments In Memory by Ryan Ochoa .................... pg. 152

# IX

Untitled by Betsy Dudash ..................................... pg. 154
Your Words by Martha Flores ............................ pg. 154
Untitled by Moon Rae ........................................ pg. 154
Broken Wings by Betsy Dudash ......................... pg. 155
Purgatory by Anna Marie Sullivan ...................... pg. 155
Untitled by Moon Rae ........................................ pg. 155
Your Light by Sabrina B .................................... pg. 156
To The Future by Sylvia B .................................. pg. 158
Societal Narrative of Love by Anabel Watson ......... pg. 159
Winds Of Change by Allyssa Arnold ..................... pg. 159
Untitled by Ruth Joy .......................................... pg. 160
Confused Pt. 2 by Maximus Ceballos ................... pg. 162
Love by Charles K. Chuckenspire ......................... pg. 163
Sticky by Jesemynn Cacka .................................. pg. 164
Vestige by Zoe Zamorano .................................... pg. 165
Good Girl by Anna Marie Sullivan ....................... pg. 165
Raw by Jana Divis ............................................. pg. 166
Fishing by Holly Thorpe ..................................... pg. 167
Touch by Kennedy Clark ..................................... pg. 168
Finally Free by Kristina Stepper ......................... pg. 168
Hair Of The Dog by C.G. Dahlin ......................... pg. 169
She Quivers by Diana Rigelman .......................... pg. 170
Ingram by Sylvia B ............................................ pg. 170
Let Love Happen by Ryan Ochoa ......................... pg. 171
The Key To My Heart by Judie Peavey .................. pg. 171
The Gift by Sabrina B ........................................ pg. 172
I Wish by Charles K. Chuckenspire ...................... pg. 174
Unfolding A Goddess by Jazmyn Jira ................... pg. 175
Unsent Flowers by Mike Morgan .......................... pg. 175
Untitled by Betsy Dudash .................................. pg. 176
Our Room by Linnea Charmaine Rigelman .......... pg. 176
Sunset Of Love by Kendra Barahona .................... pg. 176
Fiddler Crab by Ray Sharp ................................. pg. 177
Mantra by Michael Reed Schooler ....................... pg. 177
Moving In by Sabrina B ..................................... pg. 178
So Cracks The Heart by Diana Rigelman ............. pg. 180
Resignation by Ulises Navarro ............................ pg. 182
You Be A Tree by T.J. Rodriguez ......................... pg. 182
Lost And Found by Ryan Ochoa .......................... pg. 183
Relationships by Eric J. Stepper ......................... pg. 184
Untitled by Vic Tapscott .................................... pg. 185

# X

The Treehouse by Wendy Howard ........................ pg. 187
Brilliance by Anabel Watson ................................ pg. 188
The Closest Thing... by Kevin Lane Strickland ...... pg. 189
Aubade 11/8 by Mitch McCarrell ........................ pg. 190
The Young Dead Speak Ill Of... by Ray Sharp ...... pg. 190
Tetra by Anna Marie Sullivan ............................. pg. 191
Mercury by Eric W. Fotherby ............................. pg. 192
Dreams Into Darkness by Russell Babbitt ........... pg. 194
Nothing And Everything by Sylvia B .................... pg. 195
Polychromatic by Jana Divis ............................... pg. 197
Untitled by Tyler Burlingame .............................. pg. 197
Untitled by Adam Leonardini .............................. pg. 198
05/24/19 by Jon Davies ..................................... pg. 198
Insomnia by T.J. Rodriguez ................................. pg. 198
Everytiiiiiiime by Ethan Starkey .......................... pg. 199
Untitled by Ian Ford .......................................... pg. 199
Would You Like To Exchange... by Jon Davies ...... pg. 200
Restless by Gavin Johnson ................................. pg. 200
Bartender by Jesemynn Cacka ............................ pg. 201
The News From Home by Mitch McCarrell ........... pg. 202
The Python And The Seed by Faith Merz ............. pg. 204
06/13/2019 by Jon Davies ................................. pg. 209
Cider by Gary Trader .......................................... pg. 209
"Alex Hayley Wannabe Shtick". by Ben Anon ........ pg. 210
Six Hours Later by Chad Ruggles ........................ pg. 211
Big Toe by Jesemynn Cacka ................................ pg. 214
Ode To The Sleepless Night by C.G. Dahlin ......... pg. 215
Untitled by Michael Reed Schooler ..................... pg. 216

# Editor's Note

by C.G. Dahlin

This project's creation, and subsequent Vol. 2, was prompted by the notable creativity of the many people who pass through or call Wenatchee, Washington home. The Greater Wenatchee Area is what ties all of the contributing writers together. Their travels within and well beyond the valley all contribute to what substantiates what is being expressed within.

The themes and sentiments felt herein are what is carried in the hearts of the people that have breathed the air resting on the east side of the Cascades. The objective of this collection is to show the true soul and catharsis of those who have found themselves here, in one way or another.

With this considered, the undertone of this collection (poetry, short stories, and the unclassified in-between) shows what themes bring these diverse people together regardless of how their expressions and beliefs vary. This is what they naturally produce and this is what unifies them.

This collection was also assembled to counteract the conventions that modern publications typically take on, even in regards to standardized punctuation and format. None of the contributors paid a fee and there are no titled winners or honorable mentions. Those who have been featured more than others have only been so because of the sheer amount and diversity of what they submitted, while others have chosen to submit little. With this considered, this project aspires to be egalitarian in nature.

The writings you'll find herein were chosen for their thematic-ness as opposed to some convoluted concept of what is "good" writing or for the contributors' submission to a predetermined theme. Natural expression is the treasure of this work.

In this way, especially in this collection as opposed to the last volume, the reader may notice what appears to be editorial inconsistencies or maybe even misspellings. As the curator of this work, I've had the very welcomed and ever tedious responsibility of working with all of the 68 authors on an individual basis (double the amount of writers than in the last collection) to ensure the uniformity of the book did not compromise their creative vision. If you think there's been a mistake, look twice, and consider a poet's eccentricity license.

In the last volume, there was more strictly held mold in regards to formatting and punctuation. In this volume, with the many more voices considered, uniform punctuation, style, etc., opened up and offered more variation to help stratal that ever fine line of the "professional," organized and strictly maintained anthology and the genuine, unfiltered natural expressions created by all of the highly variant contributors. This collection aims to marry both, the absolute mess and anarchy of our inner experiences with the synchronicities, similarities, and often unseen uniformities of our collective existence.

In other words, this collection aspires to be as illustrative of the voices of this valley as possible, in all of their contrast, whilst maintaining a professional form. It aims to show the humanity, authenticity, and inherent creativity of the people who've happened upon the Wenatchee Valley.

I

### The Inward
by Michael Reed Schooler

It's as though we still havn't- a voice
our livelihood digging and grooving
rejoice!

laugh at the backhand
of whom
"Noise, Annoys"
For They simply can't jive
we are hung
before hoist

**Failure**
by Mitch McCarrell


All those failing poems out there. Everyone
wanting to catch a little lightning off Lowell's
old queer friend and then some. But fuck failing
it doesn't need my help.

The dead rose bush, 3 buckets full
of ruined apples, so hard to beat insects and birds,
one and a half acres, who couldn't manage
that, the two irrigation lines. I spent all summer
not getting the roof on the workshop
I started two falls ago.

The above ground swimming
pool those last bastards on the place
dug in deep and encircled with a wide deck
taking me two long hot summers to demo.

Yes, there's that novel I started
thirty-four years ago but I'm working on that.
At least the marriage came to an end and those
children raised themselves and two parents died
and managed to get themselves buried
and the bills get paid, income tax taken out
of the check like clockwork.
Nothing misfiring there.

Sitting alone yesterday after all
the day's chores had been attempted,
for a second I thought how nice it would be
to meet a woman. To kiss her and feel her lips
on mine. To hold her in my arms and romance her
and then eventually I suppose
sex would enter the picture.

Yes, there's the beginning of a disaster.
That adventure might still need living.

# Kill
by Jesemynn Cacka

Often I write poems on loose pieces of paper I can crumple in my pocket. I read to my friends the long winded, strung together sentences, like popcorn garlands no one will ever digest.

It's still unknown if it's intentional letting these entries float into space without a tether to notebooks or digital copies. I say, I'm just in a rush, but really, I've filled note-books to the brim with works I'm not proud of. Still, I let them loose, in a high wind frenzy scattering the words to landfills.

There was even a time I filled a book with sad poems about a boy who played the wolf in sheep's clothing. The book rolled beneath muddy feet of my car floor, trash stacked on top, but a pain I couldn't just throw out. The last tether to a man who never thought twice about me.

I was camping by the ocean, lulled by the shh of the sea. The cold crept in as the night tucked us close. Unprepared without kindling or knowledge of how to make fire, I re-membered the war torn book.

It didn't hurt as I ripped pages of handwritten poetry to start a flame of warmth. I did not care, about losing that work, because sometimes I pretend I'm a monk practicing the art of letting go. It's all impermanent and will eventu-ally burn away once my ashes have been scattered.

Often, I write poems, that just don't last.

## Letter To The Editor
by Russell Babbitt

I'll pay for my prose, cash out for the commas,
rewrite my romance, dissect all my traumas.

Look in the napkins, unravel the clothes,
ask Levi's for edits, and socks about prose.

People inside of this poetry bubble go aching and raking,
disturbing the rubble.

Earmark the articles, nix the conjunctions,
use line breaks and rhyme schemes to alter the function.

Why have I asked you to edit this piece?
What is the insight I'd like to receive?

Commas to periods, dashes to ands,
writing is morphing, concealed in your hands.

No need for niceties, say what you mean,
it isn't acceptance I'm trying to glean.

Tell me the errors, recite the mistakes,
turn inlets to tide pools and rivers to lakes.

Put commas and ampersands all in the mix,
beat beauty with barbells then poke it with sticks.

Contempt into malice and death to decay,
reverb to resonance, slice to filet,
And to including, these into those,
a gaggle of geese to a murder of crows

Remnants to pieces and shreds into scraps,
beers into lagers, and bullets to caps,
words into vocab and charts into graphs,
awe into wonder and chuckles to laughs.

Your input's been noted, your insight's been marked...
Next time, don't edit my work in the dark.

## The Difference Between Poems And Poetry
by Judie Peavey

A poem can be any verse with words that rhyme;
to write one doesn't take much time.
It doesn't take a lot of thought
to write a poem that can be bought.

Poetry, however, comes from the heart.
The words flow like a gentle brook right from the start.
Great poets write about their dreams.
They tell of past and future schemes.
They write about folks they love,
about the stars, the moon, and sun above.
Some write about now while others write about then.
Sometimes they write about women
and sometimes write about great men.

As for me, I'm good at rhyme
and so I do this in my spare time.


## Peace I Ask Of Thee, O River
by Linda Reid

Come sit beside the river.
It is what it was yesterday.
The sky, not the same sky,
the light, not the same light,
it is transformed.
Yesterday, fog pockets, misty dampness, daylight leaning
into twilight, but the river is what it was yesterday.

The river pays no heed to what I notice.
It is not distracted.
Journeying, flowing relentlessly,
forward motion, its only direction.
I envy that single-focused intention;
the ability to continue without distraction.

The river gives me a glimpse of creative flow.
Full attention focused on the journey and the destination.
The river offers me a chance to reflect
and feel its gentle guidance.
Renewed inspiration for a poet to keep searching
for the words to tell her story.

## The Wasting Poet
by Kevin Strickland

The Raven appears above the dread
Come to graze what is not dead
To pluck an eye out of my still dreaming head
To peck free a finger from it's death grip on the ledge
Or to perhaps gently rap and whisper some sweet rapport
From what I've heard that's what occurred over Edgar
Poe's chamber door

And that aged thrush still perched upon it's tangled
bine-stems
Flings no forever hopeful carol upon the growing gloom
But at hymns end returns all concern to the state of
Winter's plume
And away from what fruits wither on the vine

Now it's sounds absurd but in my mind
Those birds are a sign
Sent by the immortals
Meant to inspire my next line
With verse so profound both king's and commoners would
quote it
At our lord's behest I'm a guest at the palace where all
stand and hail
The Wasting Poet

Yes but mine is more than mere want for a title
And the Laureate to bestow it
What I seek is a connection to the masses
Something to say that I am here
Proof that I was alive
And the works to you which have become so endeared
Well I could say that it was I Kevin Lane Strickland who
wrote it

Yes but that brings me back to the small matter of my
empty page
To the ink that won't flow
To the ideas that won't grow and advancing age
And the more I sit and think the more I think to quit

For it is the body of my past compositions that make up
the bodies that line this very pit
And the real reason why I fear
The Raven has come to watch over it

Well Thee has certainly taken my concentration
And soon my confidence will leave me
Personified I can see it consorting in the doorway with

7

Richard Cory and Miniver Cheevy
Neither of whom would like to be me
Neither of whom would I like to be
No I would rather be known as a man who befriends men
like Gunga Din
Known for what I've done
But loved for who I've been
By fame and fortune damned than seen as kin to the likes
of them
Even if that is who I really am
Some sort of bad seed

But even bad seeds are subject to atmospheric change
Wherein the words that were once my desert now seem
inspired by all this rain
Bringing forth the flowers after flooding quick the plains
Living and surviving despite life's extremes
And always in strict accordance to the principles of my
own little pendulums swing

And I'll tell you the threshold is the damndest place for
one's will to take a stand
Yet wherein from the view of that precipice come those
moments that make a man
And any man who knows how roads diverge through
yellow wood
Knows those roads lead to nowhere for those who've
simply craned their necks and stood

And so with my pride back on the tide
I once again turn to the plight of my pen
Eager to convey both my loves and frustrations and
Less obsessed with just who's favor I'd win
And all through the night will a poet procrastinate and toil
Write read recite repeat burn the midnight oil
All to plant a seedling love in the heart of loveless soils
With the hopes that from my labor spring some
metaphorical string of perfect pearls
Or in light of hearing how my heart sings
The love of some imperfect girl

I'm certain Shakespeare did not find his form by plucking
thin his ream
More certain still he'd be a whore to his quill
To have written so many scenes
And though I may just have the habit and not the stuff of
dreams
I will always have that edge to grab at
And some semblance of soul to fling
Not to mention the esteem that anonymity brings

For all of the countless hours this craft demands it's
rewards and gains are few
In fact I scarce recall the reasoning behind why I ever
began to do what it is I do
But one thing that I've learned since the onset of this
affliction that to this day reigns true
Is the fact that poetry need not love me
She only need love you

And so
As my birds seek said buzzard-ry save my sight
take these poems in lieu
And remember that through the decades I wrote
Dasting Poetespite the fact that nobody ever knew
And how dare I compare myself to Shakespeare
well then yea I be a whore too
However, I continue to pay my dues

And Shakespeare is dead

## 09/12/2019
by Jon Davies

For thoughts to flow one must knot know into maybe. The Incan Quipu kept track of something that we haven't untangled. Weaving words around ideas that swerve serves to guide instead of define. Illuminating instead of limiting gives literature albatross wings; the type with feathers that sing with sharp turns and hum on storm fronts.

## Semi (Original)
by Ulises Navarro

Tratando de ir y no de escribir porque donde escribo me pierdo pero donde me leen ahí estaré.
Soy la sombra clara que no sale con el sol.
Fui fuego y soy de la luz la oscuridad, jugamos a la cruz en el suelo, de la medianoche al amanecer.
Me gusta ser quien soy, impredecible, especial como el karma, tarde o temprano llego, soy el cosmos de tantos colores, la sensación de amor en tu barriga,
la pureza de tus ojos.
Estamos completamente distanciados, electricidad y fuego, vértigo y caída,
los pedazos de cristal de la ventana rota.
Eres, mi ultimo cigarro, el de la suerte.
Eres, la distancia mas pequeña.
Eres, somos, soy.

## Mid (Translation)
by Ulises Navarro

Trying to go and not to write because where I write I get lost but where they read me there I'll be.
I'm the clear shadow that doesn't leave with the sunlight.
I was fire and from the light I am the darkness, we play at the cross on the ground, from midnight to sunrise.
I like to be who I am, unpredictable, special like karma, sooner or later I arrive, I am the cosmos of so many colors, the sensation of love in your stomach,
the purity of your eyes.
We are completely distanced, electricity and fire,
of vertigo and falling,
the shards from the broken window.
You are, my last cigar, the lucky one.
You are the smallest distance.
You are, we are, I am.

## Selfishness In Print
by Jon Davies

What worth would words wield without readership?
A passing authors minute fully in it is a chance at bliss.
In time I may be content with this.

If I'm content being content I hope the context is honest.
A contested context is better presented
with confidence, man.
To test text for inherent coherence is best met with a
skeptical lens.

Why does that mean that again?
The pronoun is paid to go down in place of a thing.
It may be vague and at the same time include our entire
existence.

No mocking, working with pronouns,
and my idea of floxinoxinihilipilification
as separate from having no worth.
How do you value the air and the sea?
Sell someone a glass of sand at the beach.
Have you ever purchased a single pine needle?
What good is one bee, one mosquito, or three?
Try asking the swift, a swallow,
or duckling sifting stale water for larvae.

"Pronoun is paid," is a play on professional suggesting a
role with value.

I'm not sure if this helps anyone but me.
Does that make this a selfish piece?

# II

**Motherhood**
by Taylor Lisa Bailey

She lay there, falling asleep, slow rhythmic breathing,
calming, and innocent as she crosses over into her
dreams.

Soft locks of blonde hair fall on her flushed cheeks still
burning red and hot from her tantrum.

How quickly moods change.
One moment she was crying, yelling, demanding, unable
to control how she felt or communicate to us what she
needs.

The next minute she was sleeping.

So small and fragile as if she never could do anything
wrong.

I wonder if I am wrong to allow this behavior at all.
Should I yell back or give her what she wants?
Should I be calm while her storm rages on?

She clutches her bottle like a teddy bear.
It was the only thing I could think of to calm her down.

I begin to clean up the room that felt her fury.
Picking up the things that she was strong enough to
throw.

Maybe it's time that I ask for help.
She is finally asleep so I carry her to bed.

I tuck her in.
When I'm done I kiss her forehead, carefully pull the bottle
from her grip, it is empty now.

The last drops of wine staining my mothers lips.

"Goodnight," I whisper.

"I love you."

**2:15 A.M.**
by Faith Merz

There's a humming,
a thrumming, resounding like a heartbeat;
the dogs are barking outside.

On the other side of town, past the railroad tracks,
someone turns out their light for the coming of day.

There are cats out on open roads,
someone's faking love in a hotel room,
people are living lives in the dark unaware,
and the thrumming goes on.

I think maybe Kerouac was right about the openness of
street-lit roads, the poetry in strangers, the music in the
thrumming of a town too small to remember.

Listen.
There's something to be said about not knowing
and all the beauty in fleeting encounters.
Let's take a ride, straight on through,
and cast off into the night.

### The Woman
by Gloria Piper Roberson

The woman wears everything she owns. Everything she saved from the fire in October three years ago that leaves her single-wide, fifteen-foot, silver, trailer house in ashes. Jeans, brown corduroy skirt, blue denim shirt, and two pairs of once-white cotton socks, a red silk scarf, and a green, wool sweater, more bag than sweater. It all smells of tuna fish and smoke. Underneath she does too.

The silk scarf coiling her cheeks and neck rubs against the thick, pink, knobby, burn scars it hides. She threw away her leather gloves when she found a pair of blue mittens in the woman's restroom at the 7-11 store on Long Island Boulevard. Mittens fit her burn-scarred fingers better. Her shoes fit too big and stiff. She is not their first owner.

She had a man once, Joe MacAffie. "Joey Mac," she called him and he called her, "His Honey Bear." They met at the Coffee Hut on Redondo Avenue on a windy, rainy, Saturday afternoon, in March. By summer they found they had more in common than lattes and Italian sodas. On the Fourth of July, she along with Popeye, her black Siamese cat moved out of her studio apartment on Locust Street and into Joey Mac's. He had a fifteen-foot silver house trailer parked at the Pacific Sands Trailer Park not far from The Pike Amusements.

After five years together, two miscarriages, and a stillborn son Joey Mac left her. He left his job at Crescent Paper Company in Long Beach, left the silver trailer house, and the State of California. Money was the only thing he did not leave.

Three months before the fire she lost her sewing job at Owens Pet Accessories, Inc. on East Ocean Boulevard.

"Lack of business, Honey, otherwise you know I wouldn't let you go." Mrs. Owens was as buxomly as Mae West and her voice graveled like the Madam of a whorehouse in a John Wayne movie. She handed her the paycheck. "When business picks up, Honey, I'll give you a call. In the meantime, hopefully, you have rainy day money set aside."

The woman never planned to make a career out of sewing pet collars and leashes but the job did earn her a living (if it could be called that) after Joey Mac walked out. It paid her rent space at the trailer park, it fed her and Popeye, but it poured down no rainy day money.

Before the fire she did little outside of working. Her only friend was Popeye yet she could not save him. His pitiful cries begged her to find him in the tiny laundry room. She did try. Her hands and face prove it didn't they?

Life for her then was not much different from now. Except now, she has no real home, no job, no man, and no friend. Now she shops at alley dumpsters and trashcans instead of aisles.

She wears no hat; not on this chilly Tuesday night anyway. Jacobe stole it as if he had the right. He snatched the green wool hat right off her head last night while she slept in the red sleigh on the carousel at the Pike Amusement Park. She doesn't sleep in the sleigh every night; only on Tuesdays. Mondays it is the Cup and Saucers, Wednesdays the Tilt-a-Whirl, Thursdays the Octopus, Friday she is in a Bumper Car. She only slept once in a Roller Coaster Car; she felt trapped all night by the lap handle. Once she slept in the House of Mirrors. She felt safe enough there from Jacobe, though she could not hide from her scar-faced-self.

She lives on the beach at the Pike Amusement Park. She discovers life is easier there then under the Third Street Bridge where a bed partner could be a rat or a wretch or both. Finding food is a snap. Every garbage bin is a feast. There's corn dogs, french fries, curly fries, hot dogs, hamburgers, popcorn, corn-on-the-cob, glazed donuts, speckled donuts, cotton candy. She can wash it all down with cold coffee or warm fizz-less soda pop she finds in lidded plastic cups abandoned under park benches like little puppies.

After the park closes it is no problem for her to avoid the Pike Security Guards. Jacobe is the problem. She discovers him the night she decides to sleep in the Ferris Wheel.

"Get outa here, Girlie!" His slurry words heavy with 20/20 MD wine. "The Wheels my place." He stabs his chest hard with his finger and totters unsteady as a table with uneven legs. "All of it all the time, Girlie. You find your own sweet place. Jacobe don't want no company of no kind. Especially your kind, Girlie. I've seen you before. You're enough to scare a spook in a haunted house." His smelly words spray her face. "Don't you forget it, Girlie. The Wheel's mine. Don't you forget it none!"

Jacobe, quick and quiet like a shadow, appears at the amusement park weeknights shortly after the park closes at ten o'clock and promptly after mid-night on weekends when the park stays open late. He comes with his bedroll roped over his shoulder, a plastic Pepsi bottle filled with 20/20 MD wine hooked on his belt with a piece of bent wire. On this chilly Tuesday night, Jacobe's old dreadlocks stick out from under a green wool hat like dirty garlic roots yanked up from the ground.

Jacobe plops his bedroll down on the ground by the bench near the Ferris Wheel. He peels off the hat. It drops on the bedroll. He unhooks the wire from his belt, unscrews the cap from the bottle, and folds himself down on the bench. He sticks his legs out, crosses his feet, leans back and takes three hefty swigs of wine then holds the bottle straight out in his two hands.

"Lifeisbeautiful." His words cannot get out of each other's way.

"I'mgladyourheretoshareitwithme."

He puts his lips to the label. Then he screws the cap back on and drops the bottle onto the bedroll.

He digs a ragged book of matches and a piece of chewed cigar from his burned pocket shirt and lights up. A deep drag sets him coughing. A few more drags and he leans forward, rubs the cigar out on the toe of his grimy tennis shoe, and places it back in his pocket. He grabs his bedroll by the rope, slips it on his shoulder, and shimmies up the gray frame of the Ferris Wheel like a drunken spider. Jacobe sleeps in the highest dangling seat. He wants his privacy, wants his morning view, like Joey Mac and fire, Jacobe takes what he wants.

The woman stands hatless beneath the Ferris Wheel. She removes the wire from around Jacobe's Pepsi bottle and slips it under her sweater into her shirt pocket. She unscrews the cap and toasts the bottle upward.

"Jacobe, you are a hell of a teacher. I'll give you that but only that you bastard."

She rubs the mouth of the bottle with the front of her sweater, takes a quick sip, and spits it on the ground. "I spit on you and Joey Mac. You're both no good!" Her voice crumbles.

She wipes her mouth with her sleeve then tips the bottle forward slowly. The wine flows out like an indelible line of hot purple lava. It splashes onto the asphalt, onto her shoes, up onto her jeans, and the hem of her skirt perfuming the air like the wine on a communion Sunday. She hurls the cap into space and listens to it hit the asphalt then twirl to a hollow stop. She walks away from Jacobe's wheel and drops his empty bottle into the third garbage bin she passes. She continues to the Fun House; climbs up into the smiling, giant face of Bertha the Clown, her mechanical laughter silent in her gaping mouth.

The woman reaches under her sweater and removes the bent wire from her shirt pocket. She sticks one end of it in a small hole in Bertha's lip. On the other end she hangs her green wool hat.

"You're a hell of a teacher Jacobe."

## Un Dia Con El Viejo Facundo En Las Favelas Brasileñas (Original)
by Ulises Navarro

Me acabo de dar cuenta, que la vida es tan bella, que los problemas son tan insignificantes, que somos tan pequeños y poderosos a la vez, que no importa nada más que el crecer, evolucionar, amar y seguir.

Que la vida es una escuela, la tristeza es momentánea, que el dolor es secundario, que el dinero es siempre insuficiente, que alimentar la mente y el espíritu es lo principal.

Que el único dios que debemos alabar y cuidar está en nuestros pies, la Madre Tierra es la que nos dio la vida, nos provee de comida y refugio, que es a ella la que debemos el todo.

Somos tan torpes e ilusos. ¡dios! Somos tan dichosos y no lo vemos.

Sonríe y jamás te rindas, sigue caminando, sigue, y no pares, no hay futuro, el mañana es relativo, ya que nadie te garantiza la vida en los próximos cinco minutos.

## A Day With The Old Facundo In The Brazilian Slums (Translation)
by Ulises Navarro

I just realized, that life is so beautiful, that our problems are so insignificant, that we are so tiny and powerful at the same time, that nothing else matters but growing up, evolving, loving, and continuing on.

That life is a school, sadness is momentary, that pain is secondary, that money is never enough, that feeding the mind and the soul is foremost.

That the only god that we should worship and care for is beneath our feet, Mother Earth is she whom gave us life, whom provides us with food and refuge, that it is to her to whom we owe our everything.

We are so clumsy and deluded. God! We are so fortunate and we don't see it.

Smile and never give up, keep on walking, go on, and don't stop, there is no future, tomorrow is relative, since no one guarantees your life in the next five minutes.

## Sunoco Row
by Eric W. Fotherby

Dirty Tony looked very much like the classic Italian. It was
the summer of 1967 and he had decided he was going to
take his wife on a trip to Florida in their late model, gold,
Coupe De Ville with the white convertible top. His frizzy
black and gray hair was thinning with a bald spot in the
back. He had a very hairy chest with a gold chain fully
displayed in a half-buttoned shirt. He was missing a few
teeth here and there so that when he became angry a tor-
rent of foul expletives and epitaphs would explode from
his mouth like a shotgun. He would be waving his arms
around and he would sputter and spit bubbles would be
flying. It was all haphazardly ejected onto anyone that was
unknowingly standing within a range of about six feet
from him. We were soon to discover later that he didn't
come from Italian heritage at all. We came to find out that
Dirty Tony was actually of French, Moroccan, and Jewish
heritage. All of this time he had just been putting out the
impression that he was connected to the mob just so that
he could intimidate any troublemakers in his life whenev-
er he deemed it to be necessary.

For a while he was thinking of selling his gas station in
the Detroit suburb of Warren, Michigan and opening up a
new one down in the Miami, Florida area. He would tell us
about how beautiful everything and everyone was there.
He would tell us how there were endless palm trees and
beautiful young girls in bikinis. He had a location all
picked out for his gas station near the Fontainebleau Ho-
tel which was the Mafia's showpiece Five-Star hotel way
back when in the summer of 1967. After talking to some
Real Estate Agents in Miami, Tony was visited the next
day at his motel by a couple of real Mafia mobsters. They
unkindly informed him that if he were to open a gas sta-
tion in town that he was going to have to pay eight hun-
dred a month in Protection money to them.

When Tony returned back home from his most recent
business trip/vacation he told us that all of those fucking
Wops could die and go to hell before he was going to pay
any fucking one of them any fucking Protection money! He
was so pissed off. He raged on and on and he cursed the
Mafia for days on end. His young crew was now all very
disappointed to find out that Tony wasn't really a Mafia
Don and now even worse yet that he had become involved
in a contentious relationship with the Miami Mafia! This
turn of events now spelled nothing but disaster for a
bunch of horny, hopeful, teenage boys such as us who
were planning to work for Tony in Florida. To revel and

carouse and debauch our way through the endless stretches of beaches that were full of sexy, voluptuous women wearing nothing but itsy-bitsy, teeny-weenie bikinis!

Reality then began to hit us all pretty hard. We all knew that our wild fantasy had just ended and that it was time to make up new plans and new fantasies. After dodging Tony for a couple of weeks while he was spewing his curse words and spit bubbles in all different directions he finally gave up on his plans of moving South to the white sand beaches of Miami with endless palm trees and bikinis. He talked about trying a few other places out but he finally settled back into his role and regular routine as that of "Dirty Tony, Petroleum Entrepreneur Extraordinaire!"

Things kind of eased back to normal after that. We had an ongoing wink-wink policy with people wanting to fence merchandise out of the trunks of their big luxury cars. I know that they paid Tony to do this but he never told me how much. It was probably settled mostly with merchandise. New cars were a real bargain in Detroit in those days because there were no shipping costs and lots of car dealers. Big trunks made nice merchandise displays in the parking lot of the station. The items for sale were mostly very colorful dress clothes that were being displayed. There were Ban-Lon knit shirts, some with leather fronts, a rainbow sized selection of sharkskin pants, pointy Italian leather shoes, and leather jackets. There were also watches, jewelry, custom car parts, and many auto accessories. It was come one, come all, and one of my jobs was to always be on the lookout watching the street for the Cops.

Ernie the mechanic was a short guy from Tennessee who was always smiling. He looked a lot like Burt Reynolds and had much of the same sense of humor as the celebrity. At ten p.m. he would walk across the street to Roman's grocery and buy one or two six packs of Carling Black Label beer depending on how many of us that were working that night. What we didn't know was that he had paid for it with a twenty dollar bill from the till. Then the next day when Tony said the till was short Ernie would quietly take him aside and blame it on the new guy. There always seemed to be a new guy?

My first day on the job the till was short sixty dollars but after washing my gas station pants my Mom found a washed out twenty dollar bill in my back pocket. When I went to Tony confessing my error I assumed he was going to fire me and I had accepted my fate. Instead I had now

21

become his trusted buddy. While he was grooming me to be his new crew informant Ernie was also grooming me to be his trusted best friend and confidant. Being an honest well raised Lutheran boy with a gift for the gab Ernie had dubbed me with a new nickname and from then on he always referred to me as "The Preacher!"

When I first hired on I was only fifteen years old but I had known that Tony had a reputation of paying less than a minimum wage of a dollar thirty-five to underage kids if they could keep their mouths shut. When I asked he offered me a dollar and five cents an hour plus tips and I said, "Sure, I'll take it!" From then on for the rest of the summer he paid me in cash and I was able to buy myself a fairly new 650cc Triumph motorcycle before my sixteenth birthday.

Tony had never asked me to see a Driver's License. He didn't let on but he knew that I didn't have one. He just told me to back a car out of the garage stall and to park it on the lot. I walked over to the car in the stall praying that it was an automatic transmission. I looked at the steering column and thank God, this was my lucky day! I carefully backed the sedan out and parked it and after that I was hired. I still had another test coming up that day that I didn't yet know about. When it was time for Tony to go home at five he told me that I was to drive the Jeep. To follow him to his home and then I could walk home from there which was only another block away.

Today was going to be my first stick-shift driving experience. All I knew about driving a stick shift was what I had learned from listening to my Father describing the intricacies of downshifting gears. I thought this was a do or die moment for me so I got into the Jeep and started it up. I knew that the small Jeep would be a lot easier to clutch then a full size vehicle so I was going for it. Then I saw Tony take off like a bat out of hell in his gold, Coupe De Ville with the white convertible top. Now operating on pure adrenaline alone I managed to get up to third gear and then suddenly he made a fast left turn off of Twelve Mile Rd. I didn't think I could pull off the downshift maneuver in time so I ended up going around the corner in third gear and the Jeep went up on two wheels with both tires squealing. I chased after Tony to his house and parked the Jeep in the street and gave him the keys while I unknowingly had that twenty dollar bill from the till in my back pocket. As I walked in the direction of my home I was hoping that he wasn't able to see my knees shaking uncontrollably inside of my baggy gas station pants.

### The Northwest Passage
by L. Burton Brender

i am going home; i will take my red shirt, my
toothbrush, my penknife, and a paperback novel,

i am sure i won't need much
more, it can't be that far off.

but even if it is, i can't stay here,
i am sure that this isn't the place:

here the clouds are incorrectly pale, and the
frogs croak too fast, and my face smiles all wrong.

so, i am going home. i am leaving
just as soon as i can think up a way.

ah, that's it! i shall rig a ship, i shall
rig a ship and sail the Northwest Passage

and return to those old childhood friends i've yet to
make and plans i've still to lay and loves i might fall into.

i am going home, to my better here, to that wonderful
place i distinctly remember i have never yet been

## People
by Eric J. Stepper

Smile and say, "Hi,"
to an older person in the grocery store.
It may be their only social interaction for the day.

When you want to feel good...
Make someone else feel good.

Your perspective is to be valued; so is theirs.

Be kind.
It may be rejected but the odds are in your favor.

Do you know the name of the janitor where you work?
The grocery clerk?
To know these things is the currency of a good life.

Monopolize the listening; not the telling.

Our most important duty to start the day
is our choice of attitude.

Gratitude is the fertilizer of your soul.

Be a light in someone's life today.

Regrets are never useful...
Learn; then turn the page.

The greatest advice you can give your child
is to be an example of a life well lived.

Just as a rotten apple spoils the whole bunch
a smile and a kind word can spoil a bad mood.

Argue for love instead of fairness.

We chose to emphasize how we were alike
and our differences surely waned.

Your greatest investment...
People.

## How Are You?
by Cougar Penhaligon

How am I?
Well-meaning people casually ask.
They don't really want to know!
But, dammit! I am gonna tell ya
or go crazy eternally giving courtesy answers.

I am sad I am not a Father...
I am joyful that I still have a Father!
I am sad I don't have a consort
(one to spiritually explore)...
I am joyful I don't have anyone to nag me and beat me up!

I am sad I am getting older...
I am joyful I am retired
and get to do relatively what I want!
I am happy I have almost three thousand books!
I am sad I will only read one third of them before I croak.

I am sad I have physical pains...
I am grateful to have the gift of being alive in a body!

I am happy when I can
momentarily travel free of the body.
I am joyous when the Light comes down to guide me.

I treasure that I can practice compassion
and grow my heart.
I will be sad and ecstatic
when I leave the body for good!

I treasure having good friends that pass through my life!

How are you?

# III

## Wenatchee Driving Test
by Mike Morgan

Washington State is perhaps the most diverse state in the country. This has major implications for something as simple as a driver's license test. When you take the test in Seattle, it is going to be far different depending on whether you take it downtown, in the suburbs, or in a rural community. What if you take it in Sequim or Omak or Walla Walla; the scoresheet is the same but the communities are literally all over the map.

This is a self-guided test customized for Wenatchee. If you are a new driver or just new to the area, you should use this as a guideline to get a feel for local conditions, to see if you are really ready to operate a motor vehicle in our community.

Test Outline:

Go through the usual safety checks. Buckle up, adjust mirrors, set the radio to something cool, all of that. Begin at the DL Testing Office and head north on Mission. You will soon come upon a series of confusing intersections. Merge right onto Miller and then back left onto Wenatchee Avenue.

Continue northward for a few blocks and then turn in at Wendy's. Go through the drive-thru, order a triple with the works, a chili, and coffee. A lot of attention is given lately to texting while driving as a dangerous distraction. But if you can drive with a hot cup of coffee, while eating chili, and a sloppy burger, then you are a well-seasoned, highly skilled driver.

Exit Wendy's turning left onto the Avenue. This is not a test of skill or knowledge. It is the Kobayashi-Maru no-win scenario of driving. This is a test of character. Somewhere between patience and stupidity lies a realm where anything is possible. Everyone who has ever turned left out of Wendy's has been to this realm.

Next, turn right and maneuver around the Red Barn. Head up Walnut and turn right onto Stella. Continue past Home Depot and head up the hill to Walmart. You will enter the lower side of the parking lot. Your goal is to claim a space and park within the painted lines. There will be one or two hundred open parking spaces immediately available. You may use them to practice parking within the painted lines but otherwise ignore them. Parking there would require you to walk for at least forty-five seconds before you reach the store. Instead you must score a spot within fifty feet of the building. Navigate the lot in a deliberate sweeping pattern, paying attention to the one-way traffic flow implied by the diagonal parking spaces. If this is beyond your comprehension, you are too stupid to live, much less be allowed to drive. Once you have identified a potential parking spot, proceed as quickly as possible, while avoiding pedestrians and other vehicles.

Next you must decide how to deal with the shopping cart in the middle of your chosen parking spot. You could pass by and search for another spot or get out of the car and move the cart to a corral. But those choices would do nothing to highlight your driving skills. Gently maneuver and use your bumper to nudge the cart out of your way. You now have your prized spot and the cart is neatly wedged between two other cars.

Do not exit your vehicle at this time. Shopping at Walmart in Wenatchee is a completely different topic, worthy of its own instruction manual. Back out of your prized space taking care not to collide with the driver on your bumper who is waiting to take your spot then exit the parking lot and head up Maiden Lane.

At the top of the hill is a curve that turns onto Western Avenue. The speed limit entering the curve is 25 mph. The speed limit exiting the curve is 35 mph. This implies some degree of acceleration while making a navigational correction. Even if you understand the legal implications, laws of physics are in command. If you accelerate too soon, or too dramatically, you will jump the curb, and take your place among the many who have demolished a section of the fence in front of the cemetery. Not good. Staying out of the cemetery is a worthy driving goal in any town.

Assuming you are still on course, continue on Western. You will immediately come up behind a 1984 green Buick going 20 mph with the left turn signal on. They have no intention of turning left and may not even know where they are. You must endure this for the extent of your journey on Western. Also there will be a vehicle that suddenly appears on your bumper at a distance of approximately eighteen inches; usually a black pickup with oversized tires, headlights level with your roof, and a trailer hitch that could tow the Statue of Liberty. If your car is bouncing off the ground every second or two, don't worry. Those are not speed bumps. They are a side effect of the music emanating from the pickup's speakers at maximum volume.

Do not let this increase your stress level. Soon you will encounter a roundabout, which changes all of the rules. Nobody knows exactly how to negotiate them, including you. The idea is to eliminate the dreaded left-hand turn, thereby reducing traffic congestion and collisions. But the genius who devised this convolution failed to recognize some basic concepts of logic. You may instinctively believe that the shortest distance between any two points is a straight line. Sorry, but basic geometry does not apply. To go straight, you must turn right to enter the roundabout, then reverse course one hundred-eighty degrees in a radial arc, essentially making two left turns, and then swerve back right. A left hand turn requires one right, three lefts, and then a final course correction back to the right.

Perform the prescribed maneuver necessary to continue south on Western but there is a roundabout hack that can free you from being sandwiched between the Buick and the pickup. All you have to do is swerve right and then left. Keep going left. Once in the roundabout, you have the right-of-way. You can continue perpetually in a counter-clockwise pattern until you decide when and where you want to exit. Do not follow the Buick with the flashing left turn signal. He will not remember that the roundabout was installed last year and drive straight over the middle. Stay in for an extra revolution until the pickup has gone through, and then exit. Now the pickup is tailgating the Buick and you have been freed from the sandwich. Complete vengeance is not possible because no matter how high you crank up your stereo, it is impossible to overpower the Tupac Shakur blasting from the pickup's eight inch woofers. The guy in the Buick already tried that with his John Denver cassette, to no avail. Just be satisfied that some balance has been restored to the universe.

At the next roundabout, perform the necessary maneuvers for a left turn. This will result in spilling the remainder of your coffee in your lap. It's OK. Everybody does it. Next head east. Keep in mind that speed limits in school zones are reduced during school hours. Here's the catch. Everything in between Western Avenue and Wenatchee Avenue IS a school zone. Deal with it!

When you reach Wenatchee Avenue, cut back to the north. Do not go over the bridge. East Wenatchee has a different set of driving rules; a different story for a different time.

You will soon find yourself in "downtown." Pull into one of the conveniently located diagonal parking spaces, get out, and walk around. Catch your breath. Do not go into any of the many interesting shops or restaurants. Remember the coffee incident? You look like you just peed yourself. Return to your vehicle and initiate the exit process. Here's the deal. The big truck that was following you on Western Avenue is now parked next to you, immediately to your right. There is no way in Hell to determine if a car is coming. You cannot back out of your space knowing that you are safe. This is where belief in the Force comes into play. Shift into reverse, close your eyes, and just do it. If the next approaching driver has a God fearing soul, he will let you out. But even if he is the evil dark overlord of the universe, just maybe he wants your parking space, and will still allow you to exit. In the end, you must somehow escape.

Navigate north through downtown, returning to your point of origin. If you are still alive and not in jail, pat yourself on the back. The official State test should not be a problem. Remember these principals in the future as a new Wenatchee driver:

1. Successfully navigating Wenatchee Avenue is the key to survival. There are no shortcuts due to the layout of city streets.

2. Like the big cities over the mountains, we have slow drivers and aggressive drivers, just not so many. Practice patience and forgiveness, and bolster your auto insurance.

3. Wenatchee roadways are constantly under construction in an effort to improve our quality of life. Put up with it already!

4. Watch out for cyclists, panhandlers and other species of wildlife.

5. Don't be in a hurry. Nothing is more than 10 minutes away.

6. Pay attention to one-way signs.

7. Never, ever try to drive over a snow berm.

Happy driving!

**Wrecked**
by Maximus Ceballos

Started off in Wenatchee, on the way to Chelan,
we were about to down a couple cans.
Now I feel like there's a mistake...
As I open my eyes I lose all my faith.
As we hit gravel and lose control,
all I can feel is the car begin to roll;
the screams, cries, and shock got us all on lock.

I can hear my friends in pain,
I got to do something before it's too late,
so I punch and kick the window tell I get it loose.
When I pushed open that door all I can see is the floor.

Somehow that night,
I feel like an angel was watching over us,
cause we flipped seven times, and I'm not even lying.
I remember I wasn't wearing a seatbelt
but I got everyone out
but all I hear is there pouts.

Stuff like this happens in a blink of an eye
and it's okay to cry.
All I know is that we swerved and rolled
and forever we will remember
this traumatic crazy night.
As we stumble out the car,
all I see is the crash,
and the car was smashed.

As I'm standing outside I just realize...
Damn I need a cigarette.
Maybe it will help me forget but no.
As we stand there people are watching
all I hear is them talking.
All I can think about is how we're not dead,
as I rap my coat around one of my friends,
she's just in shock, and can't talk.

And to an awareness of drivers;
crazy things can happen within seconds.
To all my friends that were with me that night;
just kick it inside and don't drive.

### March 12th, 2012
by Diana Romero

A broken mind that will last a lifetime.

Diana is a twelve year old girl who's in school along with her five year old brother Alex.

The regular routine of a starting new week. A Monday that changed their lives forever. Diana had slept through the daily alarm. For the two siblings to arrive to the bus stop on time they had little time to dress and eat. School is thirty minutes away and their home was out in the country; if they missed school it was the end for them. Mom never really liked for them to miss school since Mom always said, "Your education is your future."

The two siblings had made it to the bus stop on time and were on their way to school. Young Diana was doing her math homework when suddenly she heard screams and the moment she looked up her mind went black. She was starting to wake up only to see her childhood friend, who was sitting close to Alex, cut on the side of his head from a broken glass window. Diana rushed to get her little brother off the roof luckily; he landed on top of all the backpacks. The school bus had rolled over with more than thirty-two students on board from grades K-12.

This tragedy traumatized the two siblings especially young Diana; her injuries never had justice. Now as an adult she struggles with physical and mental health.

# Untitled
by Donovan Griggs

I live in Soap Lake. On May 16th, 2019, I drove my car one evening to Jameson Lake. My fiancé and a friend were making a late dinner. I thought I'd kill some time by going for a little drive. I had the intension of finding a new spot to fish for our plans to go fishing the next morning.

Upon arriving at Jameson Lake the transmission in my car quit. I tried keeping my car in first gear, to at least drive home, even if it was very slow. My car made it close to a half mile before everything quit.

I got out, put my flannel shirt on, to somewhat protect me from the pouring rain and slight breeze. After walking for a little over two hours, I made it back out to Highway Two\Jameson Lake Road. I went to the left towards Coulee City. After roughly a half-mile, I decided to cut up over the hills, at an angle, to make my walk home a little shorter. I went over an old, rusty barbwire fence, then up to the top of a ridge. The terrain dropped low again then back up to another ridge. My internal compass told me Coulee City should be on the other side of that ridge.

When I got to the top of that ridge my cell phone got service back. My fiancé had texted me several times, letting me know that dinner was ready, and asking where I was. I could tell by her text messages that she was getting more and more concerned so I called her. I stood still on the ridge in hope we wouldn't disconnect. I asked her to call the tow truck and have the car towed. I then told her that I had no idea when I would be home because I was walking. Suddenly a rock went out from under my right foot, causing me to fall six to eight feet, before the right side of my head impacted an enormous rock. I didn't even drop my phone. I then told her I needed immediate help, as I had just split my head open. My fiancé was now very scared and worried now.

My cell phone battery was at five percent, which goes very fast when using the flashlight on my phone. She kept me calm and told me, "Use the little battery that remained to call 911." I did as she asked. The phone was at three percent when I pressed dial. The 911 operator answered, asking for the address of the emergency, to which I responded there really isn't an address, my car broke down, I'm walking home, and just fell, and split my head, and I'll need her to locate my phone via GPS. She wasn't even able to give any response before my phone dropped below two percent and shut off.

33

My clothes were now soaked with rain, with the additional breeze, I was getting very cold. I attempted to light some dead weeds on fire, it would warm me up, and tell any EMT's, etc exactly where I was. Everything was so soaking wet from the rain; nothing would light. I just kept walking holding the side of my head as I heard coyotes off in the distance.

Finally the sun was rising; I knew I'd find a road soon. I spotted an old galvanized building from quite a distance away that pumped me full of energy and hope so I didn't stop. I arrived at the galvanized building to find nobody around. I began walking towards another road that the current road intersected with.

I was very, very cold, hungry, tired, and on the verge of throwing in the hat. That's when I noticed a white car turn onto the road I was on, at a faster than normal speed, but I was overwhelmed with joy, it was a Douglas County Sheriff Deputy. When the Deputy got to me, he stopped, jumped out of his car and said "Donovan, are you alright?" To which I responded, "I hurt," as I took my right hand off of my head. Deputy Reynolds opened the back door on his patrol vehicle, I got in his car, and buckled up. Deputy Reynolds got back in his car and told me he was into over-time and out of his jurisdiction but he'd give me a ride as far as Big Wally's in Coulee City.

When we arrived at Big Wally's, Deputy Reynolds made contact with the local EMT's in Coulee City and I went by ambulance to the emergency room in Ephrata. When I arrived, the nurse told me that my fiancé had been blowing dispatch up all night trying to get search crews out there to find me and that all staff at the Ephrata Hospital knew I'd be coming in at some point. The hospital staff kept piling warm blankets on me and gave me slipper socks. The doctor made his way in pretty quickly and put thirteen staples in the side of my head. As soon as they told me I could leave, I called a friend, whom came to get me. I got home shortly after and woke my fiancé up to let her know I was home and alright.

**The Wenatchee Curse**
by C.G. Dahlin

Soaring down the byway far out from home, long before
the destination, in the in-between, the steering wheel mal-
functions; the breaks and the accelerator too.

I'm careening downhill, trying to evade future danger, but
it's like the controls have been inverted, then regular, then
inverted again.

Panic builds in me, I can't yell loud enough at my fellow
drivers, they don't know what's happening and I can't tell
them. I'm swerving. I feel the ride starting to tip up on the
sides on these sharp curves. I know it's going down, I feel
the crash before it comes, time to let loose and turn fetal.

In the last moment, I gain enough control to miss all the
cars, but torpedoed through the side of a department
building.

*Shit, shit, shit, this is my dads car, he's gonna kill me man,*
but somehow the car's fine, just the wall is obliterated.

I crashed into a storage room. One poor, bewildered clerk
is in there, looking at me like a deer in the headlights.

I hobble up to him and say,

"Don't say a damn thing... Tell no one, they can't know.
My dad, he'll hang me from the gallows. The police, they'll
piss on me. I'm just gonna walk away, okay?"

He says nothing; he just stares at me with awe. I shake
his shoulders; he's unresponsive.

I shake him more; his body resembles a floundering
slinky.

### Homestead Bones

by Gloria Piper Roberson
*--dedicated to the Piper Homestead*

Crumbled exhaust pipes lay scattered, corroded,
and rusty-red with time.

Pitted horseshoes run nowhere in the field.

The hollow water cistern howls
like a lonely ghost at the passing wind.

The burnt-black anvil is quiet; now bored to death.

The chicken coop of broken wood and wire houses thread-
bare Goodyear tires, broken-down saddles,
and frayed reins.

Busted unnamed bottles blot the ground
with their brown, sun-filled shards,
where chickens once scratched the Earth.

Barbed wire, like a spiked and mean monster,
humps and twists and
curls through the sea of tall, dry grasses.

Nearby, a green moldy car battery,
dearly departed, lies dead.

## Coming Home
by Buddy Pierce

The leaving of the land of my birth was an abrupt, overnight event. One day I was there, the next I was not. I spread my wings in search of what every young man seeks. The return, many years later, was a slow, sporadic process, in fits and starts, as though a testing of the waters. A cautious breath on the embers of old friendships and forgotten connections. For decades, they had been hidden, buried in the ash of time, still there but dormant, waiting to be rekindled. With cupped hands, shielding and gently blowing, they sprang to life; brighter, hotter, more intense than they ever were. One came from nowhere, stood before me, as though to say, "I burn for you." That heat warmed me and caused me to burn, a fiery dance that threatened to consume whatever it touched. But all the embers were there and the pull was irresistible and if you listened closely, with heart, instead of ears, you could hear them say, "Come, join us, be one of us, be us." Like Icarus before the sun or a moth orbiting a flame, I circled, in an ever-decreasing spiral, toward a center so fiercely hot that wings of wax had no choice but to melt. I thought, "Let me reach the center, before my wings are gone."

My birth land was too low to be high country and too high to be low country. An in-between that held the best of both, the worst of both, that sat squarely between the metaphorical antithesis of Muir and Conroy. A contradiction that was intensely cold in winter, breathtakingly hot in summer, mountains so high, deserts so near, that a well thrown stone could connect the two. But it was my home and that of people I love and like a carrier pigeon, barring storm or hawk, it was there I was destined to return.

I don't know when it was that I joined the ranks of adulthood nor am I fully convinced that I have yet done so. Hopefully, there's ample time to achieve a goal so worthy, should I decide to grow up. When I'm perched atop Grownup Mountain, will I be tempted to roll back down the slope and try to steal back some of the days of my youth? If I look down, will I see the boulders that are the milestones of a noteworthy life or the chasms of failure that cut across my personal trail? Will the ascent have been worth it? I believe so; as much for the journey as the destination. I would like to think that my years away added seasoning: the spices of compassion, understanding, and tolerance. I don't think of them as lost years but more as a training camp for the upcoming season. They were preparing me through trial and joy and heartache, for better days. I feel, with all my heart, that the days ahead, will be better.

In the early times of my exodus, I found myself to be lost, in a manner of speaking. Looking back at that time, endless days of nothing, blending together into a vague, blurry mess. I'm amazed that I managed to emerge, for the most part, whole and only slightly damaged. The body that was supposed to be my temple, became a drafty tent, incapable of repelling the elements, self-abused to the point of non-existence. It would be easy to say that I was a victim but if that were true then it was of myself. And maybe, in an attempt to find our limits, to push them just short of the breaking point, we all experienced some of the same things, though many did not survive the process.

I felt compelled to mention, if briefly, those days that are behind me. For though they shaped me more than any potter shapes vessels of clay, still, they are gone, and while subject to inspection, will not suffer correction. Today, my focus is forward, to the days ahead. Days that when, in some future too far before me to know, and are gazed back upon, hopefully do not beg for correction by the simple fact that they do not need correcting. If I can live my life in such a manner then past failures become nothing more than the building blocks of a better life. That this place, these old friends, accept me, welcome me and embrace me. All of this sparks in me indescribable joy. I know that I have found the true wealth of this valley; it lies in the people. After all the gold is gone, no more diamonds to be pulled from the ground, the true wealth will remain, inexplicably drawn to this geographical spot, tied by beauty, bound by love, willing prisoners in a utopian prison.

As I stand here today, struck speechless by the beauty of the confluence of two rivers, I see this place for what it was, and what it is. I can't help but wonder what it will come of it and whether I will be a part of it, without need to shape or influence in any way, but only to observe it and love it. Now, this body is old and faded, peeling like worn out paint on a clapboard house. If you wipe away the dust and look through the windows of my eyes, into my heart, you will see everything that is me. If you look closely, you might glimpse the ending of what was me, and the beginning of what I am to become. While you may see my story and from that gather a clue as to a possible outcome, you will not see the final line, for in a story with no conclusion, it will never be written, and will always remain unfinished.

## These Are The Days
by Betsy Dudash

These are the days
of naked branches against the soft warmth of the sky,
of buds counting days till they open,
of muddy paws and muddy boots,
of hope.

These are the days
of making plans and planting seeds,
of times to come with laughter and friends,
of a year in progress,
of joy.

These are the days
of growing older but not old,
of singing out loud,
of smiling at each day,
of never giving up.

These are the days
of storms still to come,
of endless dark nights,
of a future unknown but not unexpected,
of my life.


## Home
by Diana Rigelman

Home is more than Where I grew or Where I've been.

Home is also a Who and a When.

Home doesn't happen 'til I'm with Them who live within
my heart.

## Joyful Mornings
by Eric W. Fotherby

Arising from my bed I am padding along barefoot on the hardwood floor and I am looking forward to the morning sun rising above Badger Mountain in the Eastern sky. As I walk out to the street to get the morning paper the doves all scatter about that were previously perched upon my mailbox. Having been caught using it like a cheap statue I now vow unto myself that I am going to fabricate some kind of a hostile metal contraption and use it as a deterrent to thwart the doves and their deposits of white polka dots that are being left so vigorously all over the top of my black mailbox.

Returning to the house I turn on the coffee pot and I start to smell that familiar fresh aroma. It was full of a lifetime of memories as it is wafting through my nostrils and back towards the kitchen and out into the living room. It was like a genie enticing me back from the dining room while I am opening the shades to let in the sun's rays on the indoor jungle that my wife calls her houseplants. I always make my coffee Irish style and I smoke my pipe with a bowl of Snoop Dogg's "Breakfast of Champions" and I start the Daily Crossword always trying to finish it in thirty minutes or less.

When I complete this daily ritual my mind is now feeling sharp as a tack and I am ready to begin my daily chores, starting up new projects, fixing broken things, and just making my home a little bit more better of a place to live in than it was just yesterday.

There is a Cottontail Rabbit sitting next to the Arborvitaes bushes. He makes his home underground and he looks at me while he is eating the seed tops off of some weeds on the edge of my lawn. I thank him for his contribution towards my landscaping efforts.

Phil the Pheasant recently showed up again after being gone all summer. He is a very large pheasant with a long tail and he has some very beautiful coloring. He walked on up from the neighbor's yard on an asphalt easement for a distance of about a hundred yards to our rockery out in front near the street. He eats the seeds that drop off of the flowering plants that we've planted and the bugs that he finds lurking in there. It is amazing that the coyotes in the neighborhood haven't gotten to him yet so it was especially gratifying to see him returning back here again this autumn.

Coming across the road is a flock of about twenty-five California Quail heading for the bird feeder by the shed in search of dropped seeds from little sloppy eaters. The quail walk everywhere they go and they only fly when something scares them. Yesterday we heard a loud *bam* sound crash against our picture window that has a mirror finish. A quail lay dying on the front lawn with some flapping of the wings but lay there pretty much immobile from a broken neck. He got his legs up underneath himself but he couldn't lift his torso up off of the ground and he ended up dying there in that position. The males see themselves in the window and they come crashing in to take out the competition and they end up getting knocked out or killed when they hit the glass. I call the event, "From Here to Eternity," and I call the picture window, "John Wayne!"

## Rabbit Humps
by Buddy Pierce

You may have heard me mention the Rabbit Humps and if
you're from Rock Island or maybe even from East We-
natchee you certainly know what I'm referring to. If you're
not, and you don't, let me scratch that little curiosity itch
you have going on there.

It's a place, made up of rolling, mogully, lumpy hills, at
the base of Badger Mountain. I'll continue on the assump-
tion that you know what Badger Mountain is aside from
what's implied by its descriptive name. If you don't, ask
someone. The Rabbit Humps used to be covered exclusive-
ly by sagebrush and a few rock outcroppings and still has
some but a good portion of that has been replaced by or-
chards and houses. There's a road, that heads East, out of
Rock Island, up over the Rabbit Humps, circling back,
more or less along the base of the mountain, dropping
down into East Wenatchee.

It should be noted here that people or entities made up of
people like to bunch things together and assign collective
names to them. So, this area above and including East
Wenatchee, with orchards, houses, and an airport has
been referred to as, "The Greater Wenatchee Area." To me,
that seems somewhat presumptuous, unless they're indi-
cating that it's East Wenatchee that makes Wenatchee
greater. That's a concept I can embrace but causes me to
wonder, could Wenatchee not just as easily be part of,
"The Greater East Wenatchee Area?" So, pound sand, We-
natchee, eat road! No, just kidding. I love Wenatchee and
it will always be my fallback when people scrunch their
eyebrows up and press their lips together, as I inform
them of being from Rock Island.

"I'm from Rock Island." (Eyebrows scrunch, lips press to-
gether) "That's Southeast of East Wenatchee, which is
southeast of Wenatchee." "Ahhh..."

But should I even have to mention Wenatchee? Doesn't
"East Wenatchee" automatically imply the existence of
Wenatchee? Could not most of us make that connection?
Look at me, I've completely veered away from the Rabbit
Humps, if only metaphorically! The Rabbit Humps are
home to rabbits and snakes and quail and ice caves and
clay caves. One time, in my early teens, my friends and I
stumbled upon a cave, dug into a hillside, a bank of clay.

I read a section of an interview with Lucy Keane, part of
the Rock Island Keane family, pioneers and founding fa-

thers of our little town, which incidentally, was originally known as Hammond. She alluded to a clay mine, dug and briefly operated by "Grandpa Keane." But the clay wasn't of good enough quality to have commercial value so it was abandoned. I don't believe our clay cave had anything to do with that. It went back into the hillside a ways and we explored it like young boys and sometimes girls do.

One of my earliest memories of the humps, when I was five or six, was being up there with my two oldest brothers, the twins. They took me with them to shoot a new shotgun. I didn't have to whine too much before they let me have a go at it. I put it to my shoulder, pointed it more or less straight up and let 'er rip. Then I picked myself up off the ground, swatted the dust out of my pants, and gave them the gun back. "What were you shooting at? Did you hit anything?" "Germs," said I, that being the only invisible thing I could think of that might have been floating around in front of the business end of the shotgun. If they were there I surely blew them to smithereens. The last time I was in The Greater East Wenatchee Area, my eighty-five year old brother brought that up, and we laughed.

Another time I remember, my brother, five or six years older than I was, for an afternoon, tasked with looking after me. I don't remember why and it doesn't matter to the context of the story. He and three of his friends, all brothers, took me up on the humps with them. We walked around for a while and after a period of time, we stopped in a clearing devoid of vegetation, surrounded by what to me was a dense jungle of sagebrush. And putting me in the middle of an area about ten feet in diameter they dropped the S bomb on me. "There's snakes everywhere in the sagebrush. If you wait right here and don't move you should be ok. At least you'll be able to see them coming." With that, they promptly vanished, over the hill. I can only guess that they got tired of dragging me along. I didn't remember seeing any snakes on the way in, but I was never one to take chances. Though it seemed like days it was most likely only about fifteen or twenty minutes. I doubt if he remembers it but I do and that, coupled with a particular episode of The Twilight Zone, explains my aversion to snakes. Can anyone blame me for that?

So that's the Rabbit Humps, a part of Rock Island, and a part of me. Someday, when the sagebrush is all gone, and even the orchards have been pushed out, the landscape covered by houses, and if I'm lucky enough to be around, it will still be the rabbit humps to me.

**Aubade 206**
by Mitch McCarrell

The kettle in the kitchen singing, I have risen, un-godlike,
to find the cold dawn color of morning nodding hello,
breaking above Badger Mountain.
Nothing welcoming in such thin light.

I behold the new houses that fill the once empty field
that harbored hundreds of geese in years past.
Stacked close, houses sold to strangers from the coast,
area code 206.

Already they complain to me about my projects,
stacks of old wood, barrels,
the treasures I've stored against my ruin.
Projects neither abandoned nor completed.

Forgive me but in my soul I'd like to burn them out.
Spray diesel on the walls and set those houses aflame.
Watch the weasels run for cover.

Instead when the new neighbors brace me in the
driveway, to lecture me on grace and beauty, I tell them,
"It looked like this when you signed the sale papers to buy
that place. Did you think it was going to look different
after you moved in?"

## Quaint
by L. Burton Brender

narrow streets and old fruit bins
surrounded by hills and the summer din
and pioneer sons with simple grins
live in the quiet valley home

from far away and over hill
outsiders cannot see the thrill
and with that superior air will
say it's "quaint," this valley home

i see that they just don't know
how in the still winter's snow
or when the gusty autumn blows
there's a peace in this, the valley home

and though small in size,
one mile square, herein lies
the very center where the young man flies
to the world from his simple valley home

boring, dead, and isolated?
don't you realize all the things you hated,
all the callous loneliness the city created
vanish at the county fair of the close-knit valley home?

from here i reach and touch the world
with my little town's flag unfurled
where the same circles of friends have whirled
for generations in this valley home

so, i'll take your smirk and see it through
past the urban street that's forgotten you
and show you it's not half as true
as my shadowed valley home

which, until you stand on these
sagebrush hills, 'tween pinewoods and apple trees,
you will never know the eye that sees
the world yet calls this valley home

**The Be On The Radar**
(A Tribute To Radar Station)
by Jana Divis

The people that inspire me lie within these walls.

The walls that have been carefully constructed
to shelter its sheep.

There are days I walk wondering if I am alone.
I think about this place being my
One.
Single.
Home.

The place I know I'll see the faces
that know me for who I am.

For I see you and you see me.

Thank you.

# IV

## Top Down, Bottom's Up
(Bureaucracy's Finest Hour)
by Michael Reed Schooler

Assistance is not on the way
Regrettably, union bylaws circumvent no delay
your "suggestion box" rests by the loading bay
make a referral potentially garner momentum toward
policy sway

Elusive maneuvering, treacherous, under-writ power play
psycho semantic egotist politic
frantic romantic self involved heretic
love their own leverage leave you all up a crick

Wait till tomorrow while profit share ponied up yesterday
Easements permitted lend cred
through channels down hallways and annals
where fidgety midgets fill paper with digits in disarray
Municipal whipping class
dial one

simple task fudging the black into gray appeal
or compute our upmost pursuit projection,
reflection, portray.
Cheers

Yes, cheers to that

**I Do Not Consent**
by Russell Babbitt

Money.

Money is largely satanic; a panic ensues when the lem-
mings realize they are playing games.

I'm not saying names, just pointing out frames, of crisis
it's lifeless completely deranged.

On the other hand who doesn't like a few things?

A dozen Ferraris and platinum rings.
A hedge fund and then some, a gold Christmas tree,
and all of the sex acts that fit on the screen.

Well I like some things and I'm kind of attached.
It looks like this money is a serious trap.

In a system without wisdom, a place where we pay, for
every coffee on every day, where barter gets harder,
and wider arrays of crypto are tracking us buying a J.

The bank accounts with dank amounts of cash will have a
blast, unwrapping all the presents, and discarding all the
pasts.

If you like new identities then go give mine a try; my SSN
is written on the heart of my third eye.

My credit score is just a bore, it's likely been erased,
balancing my bank account is clearly just a waste.

When you're home from work we can just tell the kids too
bad; we can't afford your Mother and she can't afford your
Dad.

**exit us**
by Greg Wright

Then God's Chosen People set out from "The Land of the Free" and "The Home of the Brave" and found themselves in the Wilderness of Sin. They set out on June twenty-sixth, two thousand fifteen. As you might expect, God's Chosen found much cause to grumble.

"If only Jesus had raptured us all Prior to Roe v. Wade," they moaned. That would have been a true celebration of life. For in those days men married women and women married men and didn't worry themselves about what men did on the side. We winked at adultery and invented no-fault divorce. We gave into marriage (and a great deal more) and ended marriage just as easily.

For marriage is almost as sacred as life itself. It says so in the party platform. God therefore rained blessing and land on home cuz that's how God works. CF: Ward and June Cleaver. Savvy?

"But now we have been led into this wilderness to be disgusted by the abominations that we all agree are the abominations. That God really and truly cannot abide. Other vices, ours in particular, are mere peccadilloes."

Then the Lord said to His Chosen, "Look. I affirm to you now, notwithstanding this wilderness, that your men can still have relations with their wives, and vice versa. Six days a week, in fact, you may still have relations. Twice even on Saturday night, if you like, because it's fun, and because... Because your women will need a break from your men at least one night a week. See that you give it to them on Sunday." God's Chosen People rejoiced and discovered that in spite of the Nine Judges of the Land they could still have relations.

Their ability to copulate had not been impaired.

Monday through Thursday, in fact, husbands coupled enthusiastically with wives. While those alone in their tents, so to speak, managed to keep their hands to themselves. Come Friday, however, Men of the Chosen got, "lit up," as they say, cuz that's how the Land of the Free rolls. While they were thus sanctimoniously inebriated they "worked late" and cruised the strip and "talked a bit" with "single folk" about the curiosities and details of the ordained nightly spousal relations. These discussions, not coincidentally, also took the form of something that mightily resembled marital relations, as you might also have guessed.

On Saturday, despite the license for multiple spousal conjugations, many of God's Chosen People, being shagged out from their Friday debauch, sat on their porches or in front of computers or other portable electronics, and wondered to themselves and aloud and especially on Social Media whether other Chosen couples were having relations three or four or maybe even five times that night and were chafed at being restricted to twice.

They also speculated freely about which friends were not having relations at all and why... Also whether, perhaps, some men were in fact having relations with other men. You know.

They vomited lustily.

On Sunday most men were just disgruntled at having "missed their chances" the night before while the women mopped brows in relief that the Sabbath was not made for Man but that men might just give it a rest. Some men, however, did indeed "give it to" their wives freely and deliberately misinterpreting the Word of the Lord.

As you might have surmised would happen, God's Chosen People once again did pretty much as they pleased after going through the motions, and by the following Monday had already forgotten what God had said just seven days prior. They returned to their griping with renewed vigor. You may have heard pastors talk about this familiar pattern.

"Ministry would be great," the pastors have said, "if it weren't for the people." They cried out to the Lord, "What should we do with these people? They are ready to stone us!"

Then the Lord said, "Leave me alone. Trust me, you don't have to tell me how stubborn and rebellious (not to mention self-righteous) my... Ahem... Chosen People are. I think I shall let my anger blaze and destroy the whole lot. Check back for results tomorrow."

The pastors replied, "Well, that would be a bit out of keeping with the whole 'predestination' bit, wouldn't it? We do see your point and your solution would certainly make our jobs a good deal easier if significantly less profitable."

The Lord heaved a heavy sigh. "Not in the mood to defend them, eh? Well, see if they can't just get two things through the thick Chosen heads that rest atop their very stiff necks. One: Freedom is a gift, not an idol to be worshiped. Two: It is more brave to obey than mind your neighbor's business. Now, get a move on with your mission, but don't expect me to be seen with you. For you lot are, frankly, an embarrassment."

The pastors went and consulted with themselves and discerned that God's message could be rephrased to better tickle their parishioners' ears and forestall another round of stoning.

So it was that God's Chosen People never learned their lesson and to this day remain In the Wilderness of Sin.

### Sand Castles
by Matthew "Suihei" Morgan

Your towers of power may rise tall,
but they must surely fall,
hollow monuments to the greatest illusion of all.

### Sanitary Insanity
by Matthew "Suihei" Morgan

This mass-infection of disconnection
has got me feelin' the need for protection.
I'm haunted by yesterday's depiction
of a future frayed in mass-fiction.

In my detection of epic disaffection
I witness the need for mass-defection,
from a system that exalts imperfection
and the total disinfection of Life.

### Mirage
by Matthew "Suihei" Morgan

To suffer is to be lost in illusion –
a shadow-play of conceptual profusions.
Feeling pleasure, feeling pain,
there is everything to lose, nothing to gain.

Our Nature is always True, always the Same,
always untainted, always untamed.
Recognize the flow, recognize the fusion,
release yourself from the mass delusion.

### Stepping Outside Pattern
by Allyssa Arnold

Hate effortlessly fuels hate
but if you can look inside and try to relate,
you'll recognize that only love can heal
this wound that we all conceal.

Take a moment to see it's so much bigger than just this,
"Me."

A new way of living starts with hearts more accepting and
giving.

## Terrorism Within The Post Office
by Eric W. Fotherby

It was the late 1970's and I was working in the largest mail processing facility in the Greater Seattle Area Post Office which was appropriately named the Terminal Annex. The windows were fenced and blacked out so that no one except those in the management offices could see outdoors. It looked like a prison and it felt like a prison to all of us for ten to twelve hours a day, six days a week with no air-conditioning. As I am working on an LSM machine typing three keys per second and reading letters on my console that go by at sixty per minute, a co-worker walks up to my chair and tells me that he just heard from the grapevine downstairs that the Seattle Bomb Squad was on the first floor. He said that they were waiting for the bomb bell to arrive to place over a cardboard box that was moving slightly and making a strange whirring noise.

We went to the supervisors and asked them to let us leave the building but they refused us by giving out mandatory orders to get back to work or be fired. We were scared of losing our jobs so we went back to work in a state of fear, frenzy, and anger!

The bomb bell arrived in about a half of an hour and it was set down over the top of the carton with a fork lift. The package was addressed to the Seattle Women's Advisory Council which was well known for their liberally biased politics which were always prominently posted in the Seattle Times. To say that their membership was overwhelmingly Lesbian was a major understatement and for that reason the Police considered this to be a totally plausible threat of attack against the Counsel. The Bomb Squad set off an explosive charge inside of the bomb bell and the cardboard box was exploded into a blackened smoking mess of debris.

Once the contents of the package had been sifted through they found that it had contained one dozen sexual devices commonly known as, "motorized dildos." Apparently someone had decided to pre-test one of the machines but forgot and left the batteries inside when they shipped it out. After the package arrived at the Annex it was dumped onto the conveyor belts which began running the packages through the system tumbling on the belts as they went. It then began dropping into the big seven feet deep cans called BMC's and an "On/Off" switch got pushed to the On position inside of the cardboard box which sent the Mailhandlers and eventually all of the Clerks upstairs into a panic. What we are talking about here is part of the dayshift and the whole swing shift crew with a total head-count of approximately twelve hundred people. That was quite a large number of people to be put in harm's way!

Anyway we later filed grievances with the Union but the Union was only seven years old at that time and so basically the Union Reps were too inexperienced and lost the grievance. Mail-handler Bob, who had always been threatening to shoot us someday from the Sears tower across the street calmly walked into the first floor manager's office the following day and turned his back to her. He then bent over and dropped his Levis with his underwear below his knees showing her the full moon! When we heard about that the entire workspace was filled with laughter and everyone was now feeling much better! That bold move committed by Bob had suddenly made him famous and he was now beloved by his co-workers, one and all. It also made him the most infamous employee with management for happily ever after! The best part of this story was the fact that Bob was never disciplined at all whatsoever for his act of rebellion because management could not fire him. He was protected by the Federal Government because of the fact that he was a Viet Nam Veteran! *I also like to think they were a little scared of him too because after all, he was nuts!*

**The Day The Music Died**
by Russell Babbitt

Foxconn was a company that had started hundreds of
years ago in China. They now owned 95 percent of the
manufacturing facilities on Earth. When I started working
there I made Iphone 300s, now, as I neared 60, I was
working on iPhone 333s.

As I sat eating lunch in the dirty, beatdown, puke green
dormitory, I heard someone say that their great grandfa-
ther once told them that there was a time without
Iphones. I don't believe that. All these fairytales about bet-
ter times seemed to be nothing more than pipe dreams.

I was sitting in the common area in our pod, eating lunch
and pontificating about the intricacies of the reincarnation
trap. A looming figure swiftly approached me and sat
across from me at the old weathered plastic table. This
pod had seen too many lives come and go to find any point
in counting them anymore. I figured he was just an old
worker, a sharecropper of sorts.

Many of them had come up from the lower dimensions
when we first discovered the gateways in the Arctic. They
were workers in this Animal Farm just like us. They may
have come here straight from the pits of Hell - but they
were assembling Iphones right next to us. They had come
here to the 3D realm in order to find work, much like ille-
gal immigrants. The only difference was that they did not
bring their families, seeing as they were disembodied
demons, they had to make a sacrifice in order to reach
this realm. Almost always that sacrifice consisted of their
loved ones. Often they were sad, lonely, empty husks of
once fearful creatures. This one looked different, he
seemed to somehow possess some relic of his humanity.

"Do you know that Charley Pride wrote, Kiss An Angel
Good Morning?" he said. "He was a black man signed to
Sun Records in the 1960's, playing next to Johnny Cash,
a colored man playing country music. Reminds me of a
Warden who used to control this realm."

He would always say "I need your support Karl, not your
acceptance." I imagine Charlie Pride didn't gain any accep-
tance, but he certainly had support.

"What in the name of God or the infinite amount of Demi-
urge characters are you talking about? Who is Johnny
Cash? What is a colored person? And what in the fuck is
music?"

56

"It's too late," he sighed, breath rolling over his dry and cracked tongue like a storm made of sandpaper. "There is no chance to save your realm now. They will be here soon..."

"Who?"

"The wraiths!" He said. "You don't know what music is, you don't know any of the legends that comprise the fundamental truths of your universe! Perhaps it would be better if I just went back and helped to destroy you. Clearly it appears you are beyond saving."

I thought this being was strangely interested in human affairs. Most demons would happily bite their lip and just wait for it to start raining fire. There was no telling what his motivations were, as if I could even trust him if he'd tell me.

"Then why in the hell do you care?" I said angrily. "You came to my lunch table to warn me of impending doom?"

"No" he said. "I came here to tell you it's too late. Time does not unfold in a linear fashion in my realm, it is vertical, not horizontal. I could see that music eventually became illegal, shunned, and mocked in your world. I just didn't know it had already happened."

"What is this music? Is it a kind of drug? Like Soma?" I questioned him as I looked into his eyes. His stale gaze still burned with fire. Weathered by the years, but not extinguished.

"No, no, it's far better than any drug," he sighed as he stared towards the clock. "It is a series of sounds, tones, and rhythms made solely for the purpose of cultivating joy, anger, frustration, love, hate, and any other feeling that you want to bring about in those that hear it. I guess that probably doesn't make sense to you, there's no way you could understand."

"Well how could I?" I said. I started to feel attacked, criticized, and belittled. Then the most beautiful thing I had ever heard and seen came out of his mouth, and what happened next became the catalyst for a wave of censorship that was worse than all of the previous ones combined.

"Here, something like this" he said as he breathed deeply into the flaming caverns that formed his lungs. "Sittin' in the mornin' sun, Well I'll be sittin' when the evening comes"

He nodded and pursed his lips together, a maneuver I had never seen before. "That's what music sounds li-" - Blllat! Blllat! A gun rang out as the alarm sounded and guards descended on his position. A flame spilled out of his mouth as he fell down to the ground, the little fire that still burned in his eyes slowly flickered out.

"Down on the ground, down on the ground!" the guards barked at me as I sunk from sitting to kneeling to kissing the floor. "Did you hear that? What in the fuck do you think you're doing here boy?" I raised my hand in sign language that I'd learned from working in assembly. I signed to him that I was deaf and after a short beating I was thrown back into my quarters.

When my children are grown and I am able to take such risks, perhaps I will be able to make some of that music he was talking about. For now though, I think I'll just dream...

### Capitalism On An Airplane
by Anabel Watson

A hierarchy of basic rights and needs are awarded
based on income.
No more space in the overhead bins?
Check your bag for free!
No, thank you, I'd rather not check my bag at all...
You can only use the bathroom in the front
if you're first class...
You want chips?
Headphones?
WiFi?
Pay us a fee and we're happy to oblige.
This is what happiness is.
This is money: unequally.
Apparently.


### Home Buyer
by L. Burton Brender

repo'd sugar jars of sweet spent
air, fare trade coffee at wall-street
margin, bargain deals on usury
loan, moaning poor by cadillac
muffled, buckled dreams under gilt price
tags, bags full of gold you'll never
own, homes SLEEK & MODERN!
for only your bones


### Ignore-ance
by Matthew "Suihei" Morgan

with apathy's curse
neglect and corruption birthed
divided we fall

## What The Tortoise Taught Me
by Sylvia B

We all know the story of the tortoise and the hare;
my story is like that but different. It involves a tortoise
and it involves a hare... I am the hare.

I thought I did everything right. I thought I was doing
everything right. I thought to win the race you have to be
fast and you have to be smart so that is what I did.

I moved fast, I worked fast, I was always going, and never
stopping. I thought I was doing what I was supposed to be
doing but then one day a tortoise showed up and I realized
that I fell so far behind.

I was too busy planning and working to realize that I was
stuck in the same place... That I wasn't moving at all...
Seeing anything at all.

Then the tortoise just shows up and the tortoise taught
me how to see beautiful things and taught me the true
meaning of life. He taught me how to stop and smell the
roses and to see the beauty that life posses.

I thought I was right. I thought I was right but I was
wrong. I thought I was doing everything right just only to
realize I fell so hard and so far behind.

To realize that my feet were in the concrete and there was
a concrete wall wrapped around my mind and I was en-
trapped in what was right but was actually wrong.
There was a world out there that I was not a part of.
A world that I did not exist in because I was too busy fo-
cusing on winning the race...

When actually there is no race and there is no finish line.
The tortoise taught me that. He taught me that the only
thing you can do is appreciate the life.

The life the Earth possesses, the trees, the mountains, the
sky, the flowers, the water. That race. The one inside our
head. If we only focus on "that race" and the finish line
and winning then we will never win.

No one will ever win.

## Clever Disguise
by Allyssa Arnold

Culturally ill; stripped of all sovereign will.
Controlled by corruption, confusion, and violence;
manifesting sickness in our bodies.
A world without connection.
Dis-ease the infection.

No awareness of Earth, Body, nor Spirit.
How do you expect to see It or hear It.
Truth behind the veil; a blatant disguise.
A world where darkness always imbues the light.
Make peace with the monster like shadows inside.

Choose to be an embodiment of (the) Divine.
You are The One you came here to find.
Your soul is yours; yours to refine.

Dive on inside and take a gaze.
The rest of the story will sort itself,
so don't wait for a heavenly sent savior
or the fear of Hell's open gates.
Heaven and Hell, both are right here,
cleverly hidden between your ears.


## Heart Smart
by Kristina Stepper

"Simplify."
"Just Say No."
"It's Okay."
But can I?

The World says:
"Go, Go, Go!"
"Free time is wasted time!"
"Take on more!"

My Heart says:
"Slow down."
"Stay in the present."
"Savor the margins."

The World's way? Chaotic Crush.
My Heart's? Pleasant Peace.

I think my Heart
Is very Smart.

**Mama Says**
by Matthew Genther

Cultivating that feminine energy.
Naturally benevolent tendencies.
Let the one in your life know that she's heavenly.
Let her be who she's meant to be.
Tell her, "That sits well with me," because Momma says,
"Females are the remedy."

My Fathers and brothers are malcontents;
taking teargas to the face just for a place they can vent.
Subconsciously crying about where their Mothers went.
The future is not something you should try to prevent and
this version of the present is not permanent.

Open your mouth for the mute;
for the rights of those who are destitute.
This is not a suggestion.
This is the reason you are breathing indisputably.
Morality is not mutable.

Masculine energy is out of balance.
It makes us riot in the streets, afraid to see evil ascending,
but this weather is of our making and the remedy is
cultivating feminine energy.
Compassion and benevolence is heavenly.

A message to my men; your purpose is
to protect the innocent,
pressurize the rage inside
and transmute that into vigilance.

Have you looked outside lately?
Our divine Mother is awakening;
manifesting herself all over,
the millions of women congregating.
Never have I ever seen anything more amazing:
five million Mothers, sisters, and daughters.
It's breathtaking.
A revolution, thousands of generations in the making, and
I'll die before I leave them forsaken!

Know that life is a toy;
a gift from your Mother so play with it.
Or...
That is what she would want;
to see her babies playing together.

**Kali**
by Katharine Kiendl

Women used to tend the hearth
as men went out and gathered the crafts.
The meats, the magic, the items, that turned their hearts
to stone.

Now women tend to hearths outside these walls.
Wild in the sticks; stirring all that ignites.
No shelter to warm, no meat to cook, no skins to cure
(except their own).

Tending the flame; anchored us in it.
A cord to our maester; a snake biting our toes.

A river can only flow and a seed can only disperse
and Kali cannot contain her war
nor could Athena deny her wit so here we stand.
(Bosom heavy with pains of the old ways.)
Lighters in hand, dry grasses at our feet,
ladders ready to burn.
No snakes left in sight.
(They wouldn't stand a chance anyway.)

We cannot baptize our bodies to this flame
but we can let the salt of our old worries
bleed through the skin making way to the pyre.

We can let that salt sit on the surface
as it crystallizes from the heat
and wipe away the disbelief that rocks
in the corners of our mouths
along with the ash that stains our skins.

We can bleed in new ways now too.
Touching our womb to our backs, channeling our walls to
only flow one direction, one course, one way for ourselves,
instead of unknown ways for others.

Through our work we can repent for all the times
we demurred in the past
and let our hearth lead us astray.
Walking through coals that blistered our feet
and drew blood from our heels.

We cannot undo what's done.
That is immortalized by the burned rock that still lays.

# V

**Whirled**
by Tony Yetter

One day when the planet was fresh and new there was
held a big meeting of all the different peoples living on this
spinning ball. They gathered as representatives of all folk.
There were those with four legs, those with two legs, those
with six legs, those with eight legs, those with no legs.
There was also those with wings, those who breathe water,
those who breathe air, and those that cared.

They filled the Maker's garden and were free to be. Each
relied on their own kind to live and survive. Those with
two legs made packs for protection from those with four
legs. Those with six legs lived in hiding from those with
eight legs. Those who breathe water swam away from
those who breathe air. It seemed everybody was happy.
Mostly. Though sometimes there is not too much happi-
ness if one with two legs is being chased by those with
four legs or if one who breathes water is jerked up into the
air by one who breathes it. Nor is the six legged happy
when trapped by the eight legged. Each survived usually
by banding in groups or making hidey-holes. Each had
their method of eating and trying not to be eaten.

Here at this meeting and on this particular day all were
together. The two legged and four legged stood together as
did those on six and eight legs. Everybody had called a
truce for this very special day and they were in harmony
with each other. They were to decide on something special
that day.

A two legged stood and said, "What do we call this thing
we live on? This land stretching as far as the eye can see
or the water that flows to different shores. The air holds
not only the blue but also those with wings."

They were gathered in a great valley and everybody started
talking at once. It was thus for a while then the one on
two legs held up there hands and said "May we please fo-
cus on why we are here?"

"Where's here?" Asked one with six legs.

"Here is where we fly," said those with wings.

"Here is where we swim," bubbled those who breathe it.

"Here is where we crawl," said those with no legs.

"Here is where we build our webs," offered those with eight legs.

"Here is where we walk," said those with four legs.

"Here is where we build our homes," shared those with two legs.

"But where is here?" Asked a young two legged.

"Well, here is the Land." Said one with four legs.

"Well, here is the Water." Insisted one who breathes it.

"Well, here is the Air." Whistled those with wings.

"So what, we call it Air-Water-Land?" Asked the little two legged.

"You mean Water-Land-Air, don't you?" Asked one who breathes water.

"No! She means Land-Air-Water," insisted one on four legs.

"No! I liked it the first way. She means Air, Land, Water," said one with wings

"That seems a little awkward," said the little two legged. "And a little long."

"What do I care about the Air or the Land? Let's name this place Water!" Insisted one who breathes it.

"No! The Land!!?" Argued one with four legs.

A winged person exclaimed, "The Air is much more important. We all need it."

"Are you kidding? Without the Land there would be no Air or Water!" Offered one with no legs. "Everywhere I crawl the Land is much more important."

"The Air is in the Water and the Water carves the Land therefore the Water is way more important," said a water breather.

"For us, too, it is the Land. That is much more important for we can hide and survive!" Said one on six legs.

"Yeah, he's right," said one with no legs.

"No! We are right!" Exclaimed those who breathes water.

"If you are right then come and join me in the Air!"
Laughed one with wings.

The one who breathes water scowled at him. The folks
were starting to get angry and demanding. Finally one
with two legs, her eyes shining with reason, raised her
hands again for silence. Reluctantly they all complied.

"What we need is one word to describe it all. I have an
idea," offered the one with two legs.

"What makes your idea important?" Asked one with four
legs.

"Well, it could apply to all of us! The Maker says that this
is a ball that "whirls through the night," right? Asked the
one with two legs.

"So?" said one with four legs.

"So let's call it the Whirled!" Smiled the one with two legs.

"The Whirled?" Asked the one with four legs. "I can't argue
against that."

"That is very interesting," said one who breathes water.
"The Whirled? Hmm, the water whirls like it is alive."

"The Whirled, huh?" Asked one with no legs. He went on,
"I like it! It is very creative I think."

"Yes, very!" Said one with six legs. "It can be a small
Whirled for us little folk and a big Whirled for the rest of
you."

"Sounds kind of fun, too." Said the young one with two
legs. "My dad whirls me. I love it!"

"The wind whirls me," said one with wings.

"The current whirls me," laughed one who breathes water.

"Let's do it!" Said the one with two legs. "Let's call it the
Whirled like we all are doing now."

A resounding, "Yes," went around.
Everybody agreed and went around saying "The Whirled"
as much as they could.

"We are the Whirled," became the slogan for the day and as the meeting adjourned they began to leave taking the Whirled with them.

Then a little voice from below came rising up, "It should be what we all agree on  right?"

"Yes," said the one with two legs. Those leaving stopped to listen.

"I think you are all wrong. It already has a name. The Maker named us Earthworms so therefore the maker wants it called the Earth." Argued the Earthworm. "Did the Maker call any of you the Whirled? I think not! The answer is clear; it is the Earth not the Whirled."

"The Earth?!" Laughed the one with two legs. "I think the Whirled is much more descriptive.

"But what about the Maker?" Asked the earthworm.

"We are free to be," smiled one with eight legs. "Besides you would be better as Whirled Worm anyway"

"Yes!" Laughed the one with two legs, "The Earth! That just sounds silly. We'll see which one lasts through the eons of time. Our offspring will be here and calling it their favorite: either the Earth or the Whirled. We shall see then what it is called."

So, look around you young two legged. What do your parents call it? What do you call it?

What do you suppose the other folks think? What is more popular among those with two legs, four legs, six legs, eight legs, no legs. Those with wings? Those that breathe the water? The air? What was passed down among their kind? The Earthworms still call it the Earth as do a few Bookworms. To most of us it has become the Whirled and the truth of it has passed with those who listen and understand...

For me it is the Whirled for every once in a while it whirls me too fast and I fall down. Then I land on the Earth and understand exactly where I am.

## Sink Me Into The Earth
by Anabel Watson

Sink me into the Earth.
Sink me into a song.
To a place where I love, where I feel, where I breathe.
A place to truly belong.

Swirl me into the stars.
Wash me into the sea.
Dance me into a cloud of pink, where I think, where I flow.
Where I know I can be.

Land me at last in the woods.
Repair and relax and relief.
With the world set aside, for a time, for a while.
Talk with me.
Share with me.
Learn with me.
Speak.

Grow with me; stay with me.
Please.
Awash and away with our lives gone astray.
Who knows where we'll go if we fall off the road and return
to a state where we know we are free?
Nobody ever can know.
Only the love, the existence, the truth.
If we are all one and we care and we merge
we'll recover ourselves and relinquish our proof.

Sink me into the Earth.
Sink me into a song.
Slowly and softly.
Intent and profound.
Sing with the world as it whirls along.

## Thresholds
by Linda Reid

There is a threshold between what's inside of me
and what's outside.
That threshold keeps changing depending
on my perspective.
My threshold might be my eyes.
Are they looking outward at the world around me
or inward at my own thoughts?
My threshold might be my mouth.
Am I connecting with people or talking to my inside self?
My threshold might be my ears.
Am I listening to the noise of the world or listening to the
music in my soul?


## Palos Verdes Blue
by Gavin Johnson

Tidal forces facing death, begin anew with every breath,
life cannot stop progress, love until we know what's next,
fly away with me; away & see, a way at sea.

With you & me, dreams fluttering, wings glisten in mist,
lifting to unknown, pushing against the pull,
fulfilling thoughts, wave after wave,
tongues sail the ocean, arriving on a voice;

across the world, the wind carried you,
from breathes of men, her whisper beneath your wings,
the moonlight rises & falling in time,
a lighthouse disappears
as the sun draws near.

Two see sights, emotions of a bay;
skin-tone grounds, slowly tide down.

Lips of lost languages, find grace upon the pane,
floating on in life, Palos Verdes Blue; it's you.

## Man On The Moon
by Faith Merz

I come outside, to sit, to think,
as many have before me.

Staring up at the sky, a Man stares idly back,
and it makes me wonder.

Does the Man on the Moon watch?
With eyes made of stardust the passing of man
as centuries go by?

Has He seen mountains form and the earth shift;
forests grow and rivers bend?

With a knowledge untouched by time
does he realize His antiquity as something
older than God?

Ancient man in the sky there on His lunar throne.
He will watch long after I am gone.


## moonpearl
by Ray Sharp

the moon is a solitary pearl
with a dumbstruck simpleton's smile
curled around the tiny grain
of my solipsismal dreams

## The One Who Walks
by C.G. Dahlin

The one who walks in the eye of the storm,
moving as quickly as the undulating circumventing,
wears the out-suing lighting.

Crackles like tassels on his black hat
as dark as night and as radiant as the sun's heart.
The demeanor is weighted
but as playful as a dangling feather.

The whips and the whirls far beyond
but as felt as in the zenith.

The behemoth voice, quiet here, in the eye,
the esoteric stills, the exoteric tremble.

Reverberations, the time of preconceived promulgation.
Rain plummeting in the pattern of the hassles
he wears with his black hat.

Inconceivable, but somehow mundanely believable,
the tale/tail of the celestial snake slipping through
terrestrial dirt.

Havoc in a halo, the one who walks has joined our midst.
Walking in-between chocolate skies, plasmic karma,
dismantling manly machinations,
dissolving discordant buzzing
stored up in the day's air.

Despair on the face of the uninitiated,
run, run, run,
and not witness and learn from the one who walks.

These waves can kill,
if you don't know how to ride them.

# Rain
by Sylvia B

I am full of rain.
The clouds lie next to my heart.
My hair resembles the night.
My eyes are the murky color of dirt
with a touch of green and blue.
My eyes sometimes leak just like your kitchen pipe
but it's nothing to be upset about.

My heart sometimes feels cold just
like the ground you walk on
but some things take longer to warm up.

My eyes sometimes look dead
just like the graveyard
but the dead aren't actually dead.

Sometimes I can't help but let the tears fall
and sometimes it feels like it's always raining.

It seems as if there is no shelter from the storm
raging on on the inside and manifesting on the outside.

I can't help where my tears fall or when they fall.
Just like how you can't help but appreciate the sun.
No one is to blame here the rain comes and goes.

It just lives inside me.
I so badly wanted to be the rain.
I have now become the rain
and I still cast no judgement upon the rain.
Cast no judgement on no one.

I feel the rain and I am the rain
and there is no one to blame.

**Poemkus\***
by Eric J. Stepper

*when it rains too much,*
worms come out to perish
*on bleak, cold streets and driveways*
is this really God's way?
our thoughts are not His thoughts
His plans a mystery
*it makes sense to God.*

---

*the river runs strong*
flowing without heed or need
*unyielding to our tense will*
cleansing the earth
Mother Nature's transport
transforming life
*and bringing life hope.*

---

*rain jumps to the earth*
quenching the winter-starved ground
*green hope abounds all around*
seeds listening,
earthworms at the ready,
Mother Nature harkens
*sweet cycle renews.*


**Listen**
by Faith Merz

It's in the woods where I found things;
I forgot something down the road.

The winter prayers have come again
where beaten paths go unknown.

The bow of a pine breaks in the distance.

Somewhere beyond the safety of trees
lies the answer to a question I never thought to ask.

## The Mother's Song
by C.G. Dahlin

She came to me in the end of night
wearing the stems and leaves of a sword fern,
adorned in cockle shells, her hair sprinkling black sands,
her eyes like moons, her hands swaying and caressing like
the rolling mounds past dry gulch.

She came to me after as the birds started singing,
when the winds took a gasp, when I thought the dreams
would finally come.

She smelt of pine and morning dew,
her nails are twisted thistles
her voice unused,
yet somehow I knew it as poised and graceful.

She held me like she was swooning her child,
and put me down onto the waking ground
and softly pushed me in, as if the soil was yawning,
the grass folded around me, swaddling me into its womb.

And I was amongst the tomb where most dead men lay,
amidst the worms, vermin, and fungus,
and she sang to me there, and I knew it was her voice
though I thought I'd never heard it.

The womb started to jostle, constricting the space,
as I grew smaller within it, smaller and smaller
and smaller yet, until I was a speck of black sand
that sat placid for an immeasurable while, I panicked not,
because she still sang to me.

And somehow I started to bubble, and froth, and congeal
my portions became amorphous, my dimensions wavering,
I remember thinking, "It's painful to become."

And from here I became a seed,
and water showered down to me,
quenching and stretching and flexing my ends...
I broke the ground I entered,
the sweet light meeting my face,
I saw it as I've never seen it before, its rays, its spectra,
and in its beauty I grew, I grew to meet it,
I grew to better know it.
I became strong and beautiful,
my brothers and sisters, side by side alongside me.
We stretched and felt the wind's sigh of relief
as we reveled in the actualization
that we had become notes of our Mother's song.

75

**The Moon And The Star**
by Wendy Howard

Near the very end of her life, the old woman spoke it out loud, "I'm in Love with the Moon."

What can I do? What gift would be fitting? I'm like a wrinkled ant that crawls in the dirt sometimes looking up...

She thought and thought... Then she decided.

It wasn't easy for her but she went to four different drugstores over four different days and bought out complete lots till she was satisfied she had enough.

Then on the evening of the full Moon, in the twilight's velvet, she spread a blanket and feather pillow, with another heavy blanket on top. She placed mirrors all around her outline. From the ground it didn't look like much. She laid down to settle in and wait. The breezes blew up and died back. The Stars began to increase their enthusiasm and wink back at her delighted in her plan. She shivered and snuggled in deeper, blanket over her mouth and nose, but eyes watching the night. The Moon, she rose, she sang her song, Rosebud mouth, sincere and lovely.

"Oh," the old woman wept, "this night, this night, She is perfection!"

The Moon rose higher and nodded to the Stars, looking down at the ant world below her. Then the edges of her radiance, the hem of her astral gown, caught and reflected in the many reflecting mirrors. Carefully and tightly organized around the old women's body were mirrored compacts and cheap plastic hand mirrors. They became illuminated. Animated. Alive with her pearly splendor. The Moon saw herself reflected and wove all songs together.

She smiled down on Emily and said, "The oceans, rivers, and lakes show me this graciousness but not humans. So kind of you Emily, to give me this glimpse."

The radiance electrified Emily's outline. Her skin, luminous and pearly now too.

"I would join you," Emily whispered. "I'm so lonely. So lonely down here."

...She found herself singing, the music enveloping her, enfolding her. She was lifted and embraced by the softest most tender breeze. The breath of the Moon...

Now her eyes closed as she effervesced upward. She could see the whole of the night sky. Her heart warmed, her breath came so easily, so fully. She felt at home now, up in the Stars, up in the heights of the sky.

When they found her body, they stood around, taking pictures, writing their reports, preparing to take her away. The Sun blinding the blind as it reflected off the many mirrors.

"Bizarre," said one and they all shook their heads. The ambulance doors slammed and one by one they all left.

The yard was now quiet... The sun slipping down. The breezes blew up and died back.

...The kindness of the empty blue sky shone in the little mirrors scattered and arranged loosely on the grass in the shape of a Star...

## Ice Tear
by Kendra Barahona

Walking.
Moving.
Cold air hitting my face.
Snow crushing under my feet.
The moon shining like a star.
Sadness all around me.
Cries filling the air.
Silence.
A tear.
An Ice Tear.
Running down my face.


## Fate A Waiting Game
by Anabel Watson

If we follow the path of moonbeams.
A trick of the light.
A sort of delightful charm.
Charmed for the rays might land, glistening from where
we stand, on a shore of shadowy harm.
You cannot see from the distant shore.
You can only wonder under a moon that sees it all.


## Early One Winter Morning
by Gloria Piper Roberson

Before the light of day reveals her,
used, glistening, and stripped,
Henry leaves their bed, their room,
their aged-old, white brick house freckled with red moss.

She stands outside trembling in the frosty air.
A naked fence post against the dawning countryside.
Her abandoned arms tuck beneath her breasts;
tips hard as walnut shells.

Her auburn hair tangled like thee empty branches
of the Buttonwood tree on the winter hill.
She turns, walks into the house, then slams the door
against the cold.

Her heart snaps like bed sheets on the clothesline.

**Little Ghosts**
by Lorna Osborne

I remember summer mornings at the ocean,
the cabin, small, with room for two or four.
Fluffy beds with iron heads, hand made quilts, and
shelves of books, some read.

The salt air filling up my breath,
tides reaching and receding,
and an eagle soaring on the misty thread.

There were also wild grasses and shaded boughs,
hot with sun, infused, and tall.


**Untitled**
by Vic Tapscott

On the river, all is silent.
I can hear in the distance the call of a loon
and as I watch, a mallard and family paddle past.

I sit very still and they move on
unconcerned at how close to me they come.
The rocks move slightly under my feet
as I pause at the river's edge.

I walk into the water.
It closes over my head.
A mallard and family paddle past.
A loon calls but no one hears.
On the river, all is silent.

### Volver A Ver (Original)
by Ulises Navarro

Y fue como ver por primera vez, estaban de frente, y como no verlos si fueron siempre lo único en mi camino. Sus voces similares, pero con aura distinta y abrí los ojos y de verdad vi con la claridad desea y como no sonreír si la oscuridad desapareció.

Y comencé a caminar con paso distinto, logre sentir con mis pies descalzos el suave pastizal, y diferenciar la rudeza del terreno y la suavidad.


### To See Again (Translation)
by Ulises Navarro

And it was like seeing for the first time, they were in front, and how could I not see them if they were always the only thing in my path. Their voices similar, but with a distinct aura and I opened my eyes and truly saw with such clarity and how could I not smile if all darkness had faded.

And I started to walk with a different stride, with my bare feet I was now able to feel the soft grass, and differentiate the roughness of the ground from the softness.


### Miraculous Disentropy
by Ray Sharp

Watch a bird gathering
the smallest winterfallen twigs
one by one to fly them
to a crotch of limb and trunk
high in a stillbare tree.

Thus are the scatterlings
interwoven in the very tree
from whence they were blown,
the tendency toward disorder
overcome in the bird's design.
Take an iceground pebble

from a moraine and carry it
up a mountain. Balance it
upon an improbable cairn.
Pick up a weathered bird's nest.

Hold it in the palm of your wonder.

**His Grace**
by Gloria Piper Roberson

I see him dignified in the ice-crusted lake.
He stands hushed in the dreary-cold.

Bedeck his stately head:
antlers huge, brown, spread wide as shields.
Each breath a mist of lace;
icy drops stick to the fringe of his chin.

Then, a king, he glides his fur-caped self deeper
into the freezing waters.

He dips his face easy into the frosty wetness to drink;
to chomp on the drowned grasses.
He raises festooned with greens.

Glorious.

Bravura.

He searches for her with the hairs of his quivering ears;
with the sniff of his noble nose.
He stares as if death is his holding, holding, holding.

Then, lifting skyward his muzzle, dripping, shiny,
he bursts out his bugling cry.


**Blue Planet**
by Dalila Villamil

Unique beauty!
Majestic, colorful, and musical.
Floating palace at a point strategically designed.
It rests and moves with such naturalness.
It lightens and darkens harmoniously.
It welcomes life and gives in to all our whims.
It protects us from external threats
with its celestial layers.
It adjusts its limbs when we extract its blood...
Our home, our greatest treasure
and here we are, doing evil after evil.
What cruelty!

## Mother (Nature), Can You Hear My Cry?
by Sylvia B

Whenever I feel like dying,
like I am the equivalent of death,
I remember the trees,
I remember the forest,
I remember the flowers and the water.

When there is a forest fire
and the trees get burnt some still stand.
When fall comes and the leaves fall off they grow back.
When the water freezes over it still flows.
When winter comes, the flowers still bloom,
the trees still stand.

I will be like nature.
I will still stand.
I am still here.

"Dying does not mean death but rebirth.
I die every night and I am reborn in the morning."

I refuse to fall.

I will be the tree that grows tall.
The flower that comes back in the spring.
In the fall, I may lose some things,
but not everything is lost,
just gone for awhile.

I will be reborn come spring.
I refuse to freeze over and not flow at all.

# VI

## Double Body
by Dalila Villamil

Starting from quantum theory (the theory of the very small), objects, plants, animals, and humans are surrounded by a biomagnetic or luminous field we cannot see but can be captured by photography. This light, aura or subtle energy that surrounds us is known as the electromagnetic body or double body.

It's amazing to think energy has color, it's a rainbow. Every rainbow living being transmits light. We are an energetic flow in ellipsoid form or as an egg and our vibrations vary according to the colors that surround us. Some hold the idea that the auric field determines physical health through the chakras or energetic nuclei that are in the human body. It is also said that intuition emanates from this double body. Although materialistic skeptics do not believe this empirical knowledge, there is an increasing interest in studying this topic.

Finally, I think that studying the human energetic anatomy is exciting and crucial if we want a more spiritual society.


## Always + Never
by Matthew Genther

Mourning the loss of something temporary, I realize that I am unable to fathom the implications of always, nor can I imagine anything as brief as never.

How can a finite being such as I use these words in a sentence and not "Zero Sum" immediately after?

Perhaps there is something greater in us than what my own finality allows me to see.

A connection that can only be severed by a mind powerful enough to use words of which it does not know the meaning.

Do I believe in forever?

Do we?

**The Twisted Stems Of Spring Time's Thistle**
by Kevin Lane Strickland

Tumbleweed,
by what way have you found this post,
become trapped between the wire and the wind?
What dance across the sands has left you
tangled in the barbs, has left your fettered spirit
unsettled upon this patch of Earth?
To what oblivion has chance cast you
since the days of your green death;
since summer's gusts snapped
the twisted stems of spring time's thistle?
To what fortune might you have ventured or,
nature so carelessly tossed,
if likewise lost our paths had never crossed?
If you had a mind how would it define
this life designed to scatter ties?
And as I will end where you began, do tell,
what will fall before my eyes?
As I recall beware the future
for the past has been unkind,
each year, each month, each week, each day, intertwined.
Dread locked in the complexities of what it means to be
is the mystery of exactly what connects you to me.

The more I trace your tawny twig
the more cause I have to reflect,
for rarely, randomly, nor ever by dead reckoning
do lives such as ours intersect.
Somewhat inspired by such revelation
there came a rush of rhymes lines filled with alliteration.
And so it was that I began to unravel thee, carefully.
I took you home with me.
My plan,
to promptly compose the grandest ode upon thee!
But as my muse grew deeper I slipped into a slumber
thick with thoughts of days lost in drink and smoke.

I awoke to a clamber,
Earth chatter, chime and shutter,
and wayside, where once together
we were bound and broke.
Never again to be moved by the wind
nor consumed by the growth of a weed,
but forever astonished at the depths of man's folly
and the mindless evolution of
the seed.

## Moonlit Saunter
by Allyssa Arnold

While the world was resting
I walked alone with you
under a vibrantly bright full moon
with a halo, in the most brilliant, piercing blue.

The animals sang.
The leaves and trees danced.

For a moment the whole world fell away.
My heart unfroze.

I remembered again.
Why...

I felt again.
Why...

Nothing.
No.
Thing.
Yet so here.
So alive.

All just one infinite connection.
Experience and play.

A fabric cloth painted with eternity.
An Infinite dream from the most brilliant Mind.

we Are.
I Am.
Eternal.
I Am.
we Are.

ONE.

**Sunday, March 6th, 2005**
by Cougar Penhaligon

I came out of a core shaking Dream Vision at 4:33 this morning!

I have always imagined the Big Bang from the perspective of being an outside observer looking toward the center, seeing the explosion and then the wave of energy and mass expanding ever outward creating a sphere (or egg) of time and space.

This morning was different. I was given a Dream Vision in which instead of being a witness outside Creation, I was a direct participant in it, as we all were! I witnessed how we *became* Creation. I witnessed how we then took part in our immediately continuing Creation and how we tried at first to contain the fire that spread out everywhere and in failing in this endeavor, moved with it in a completely natural fashion!!! It was beautiful and electrifying! I am vibrating strongly now! My entire bedroom is vibrant with energy as I try to ignore it and concentrate on my writing before I forget! I came out of the Dream Vision before we created too much History/Herstory so I would not lose the important beginning but I am losing some of the Divine Reason's behind it. Everything was right there at the Beginning! If we can go back and continue reliving this moment, we can retrieve it all! I find myself oooing and ahhhing out loud! Total memory of Creation almost stayed with me! Later, it is 4:44 a.m. when I finish the whirlwind of my jotted notes striking the paper with concentrated purpose.

My first challenge right now is knowing that just by putting this wisdom into any kind of words is changing this spatially expanding experience into a one-thought-at-a-time linear experience. Also, any description of my observed surroundings is very limiting toward the true sense of what that reality IS. But, we gotta do what we gotta do, so here goes nothing (or everything).

In The Beginning was the VOID, before thought, before mind, before time was created and before any physicality.

In The Beginning there was Great Divine LOVE in that Void. Consciousness was totally immersed in that Great Divine Love in the Void.

Our Consciousness. One Consciousness.

Actually, this state existed before our understanding of The Beginning in a place called Eternity. Also, this IS before The Beginning. Eternity is NOW and always IS. Eternity IS after The End as well, beyond the Alpha and the Omega. The smokey vapor of Duality intentionally clouds our eyes from perceiving Eternity most of the time.

The VOID is not Nothingness. The Void is not empty nor is it full. It is a spacious state of BEING beyond time and number. The VOID is not a scary place. My limited mind likes to think it is closest described as, "No mind, all heart." It is closest to the heart of the deepest meditation. There is also something behind the Void but that is another tale for another time once we have taken full ownership of our latent Divinity. How may we even speak of this Reality beyond the Void if we don't even understand The Void yet? I only suggest it now as a promise of something more. This is our Second Great Promise because we are ever growing.

In The Beginning we were all one in that Divine Love but that was not enough. There was a promise! We were sent out all at once to fulfill that First Great Promise. The flood gates were opened. All of the above Eternity that we lived and dwelled in became a remote memory during the first immediate moment created by that Divinity. Remember, there was no mind (created) yet. There was only LOVE. There had been no Separation between us, until now.

In that First Moment After Forever, The Mother/Father God was created in the pouring out split of Eternal Divinity into Temporal Duality. The Vast Eternal Ocean of Love spills out into two streams, creating Duality. I became aware of myself in a beautiful shop full of carvings and sculptures and designs. I was also simultaneously aware that I was all men and Cougar at the same time. There was a beautiful woman in the shop who was all women and inside her there was a woman I knew as Kamilah who was the caretaker of the shop. I knew she was me and I wanted to reach out to touch that part of me that had been separated from me. In the mere action of reaching out for her, the shop caught fire. I guess you can say that our desire for each other in this new realm was inherently explosive. We had been closer than close. We had been One. In The First Moment she had been taken away from me and now all I wanted to do was to protect her and the shop from the fire that started to spread.

In The Second Moment After Forever, I discovered the fire seeped into every crack and design. It could not be stopped by my will as was once naturally expected since we were emerging away from the source of our Power! I simultaneously saw ourselves being spit up into many many candles of light, male and female. We were becoming Individual Souls. We had tried to stop this fire we had felt was an accident. It was no accident but we had no memory to remember that. We were only trying to protect ourselves and this beautiful shop. We had been One and now we must split and yet still desire to keep some semblance of being One.

In The Third Moment After Forever, we saw the fire could not be contained by our will, so I focussed my energy onto a wall of the shop and created a Matrix out of the Light and Dark which was given to us in the shop. As I did this, I saw the others do this as well. We were falling apart (expanding) rapidly into multiple directions and this Matrix did contain the fire in a sense: The Matrix was becoming the three dimensional fabric of the Universe that also contained the fire.

In The Fourth Moment After Forever, we realized we were splitting into almost infinite numbers and into almost infinite directions. We were compelled not to split yet we were also compelled to split. Thus the twin laws of gravity and expansion were recognized. We were discovering our now dual nature. There was no stopping it. So we acted in Creation to maintain some kind of order and we "ordered" things at each level as we came down into further separation. We attached ourselves to the Matrix and now were connected by those cords of Light and Dark. We watched ourselves become shadow with light around our shells and lightness inside us as well. In this moment we created Thought but saw Thought was separating us as well. We solved that dilemma by creating and connecting with deep empathy through the Web Of Life, the Matrix. Now came the time when things would be thought and understood with the mind that was created. The high level of God-ness slipped away from us very quickly. We had been compelled to form thought to protect our naked Souls and to preserve our consciousness as individuals as we fell into the Matrix united with empathy. Perhaps this is the source from where the diluted Story of The Fall came, with the Tree of Knowledge of Good and Evil (or duality).

I came out of the Visionary State at this point, as to not get lost in thought, quite literally! I came out of The Dreaming and back into this world (Our Dream) and found myself in bed. This experience was amazing! It IS amazing!!! We were/are all in this creation together and we all beheld profound joy in this process. We were working exactly in line with Divine Will! We were not cast out for doing anything wrong! We were guided into it by the Most Profound Divine Love for our future growth into becoming more than we ever were! How things get so twisted while we and the planet travel through time and space and the rise and fall of many civilizations. Only true Visionary States guided by Higher Power can bring us back to the Truth about us! To heal us! To make us Whole. To eventually make us ONE again. Then we will be ready for the adventure of The Second Great Promise!

To recap:

In The First Moment After Forever, The ONE split forth into the dual power of male and female, what some religions may see as Adam and Eve and what some may see as the Mother/Father God. Time begins.

In The Second Moment After Forever, the God/dess brings forth into expanding space almost infinite Seedlings originally from The One Soul.

In The Third Moment After Forever, the Matrix is created from the elements of Light and Dark. The Tibetans called this Matrix The Light Web of Life. The Native Americans call this The Web of Life.

In The Fourth Moment After Forever, Mind/Thought was created. Soul descended and was wrapped in a sheath or light body, the Mind/thought body.

In The Fifth Moment After Forever, Empathy and emotions were created. Soul descended and was wrapped in this empathy/emotional sheath also.

In The Sixth Moment After Forever, the Earth was created and Soul came down and was sheathed in a physical body.

In The Seventh Moment After Forever, I rest my case and my pen!!! Whew!

In The Disappearance Of The Universe, which is heavily based on The Course In Miracles, Gary Renard (I call him Saint Benard in jest, a hound after God) repeats claims that God did not create the Universe; that WE created the Universe, so even though I could not resist the Sacred Biblical pun on the Seventh Moment (It fell right into my lap! Honest!) my Seventh Moment does bring up a major issue for discussion on our true relationship with God.

## Mystical Path
by Allyssa Arnold

How easily lines become blurred.
Losing my mind or finding it?
Mistakes become the gifts of growth.
Pain, tests of true character.

I walk this life with one foot here.
Earthbound; a place to feel.
Joy, pain, grace, and blunder.

The other foot a bit adrift.
Dancing in the ecstatic Voidness.
Mystery, bliss, infinite, and wild;
completely full and Nothingness.

I'm never lost and never home,
a being out to *souly* roam,
neither here nor fully there,
yet, eternally everywhere.

Close your eyes child.
Ask for the Guidance
then wait in stillness and silence
until you recall the purpose
of your soul assignment.


## The Thought
by Dalila Villamil

The thought is an impulse of energy and information that comes out of the unified field that structures and engenders all the forces of nature and is experienced as material reality. It is curious since the thought (mind or psychism) operates in the brain but it is not in the brain.

The thoughts come from the source and appear in our consciousness because we are the result of the laws of the universe. In this dynamic we can feel, smell, hear, observe, walk, talk, etc., because everything originates from thought, in fact, in writing is the freshness of thought! In this sense, the great wonder of the human being will be to know us deeply to evolve through thought.

Lastly, it is good to take care of and love every bit of our being by thought.

### Shadow Work
by Charles K. Chuckenspire

My shadow and I, we work together.
She is the draft and I am the feather.

My shadow is a showoff which is why I take the stage.
An esoteric know-it-all so I often play the sage.

My shadow is my sister, partner, friend, and sinner.
My shadow shouts what I know when I am too afraid.

I witness others squelching theirs;
the power of their wholeness.
They punish their uniqueness
and glorify their dullness.

I love giving unsolicited advice
but when I'm told not to do something I'll often try it twice.

And this isn't because I don't believe them it's because I
want to see for myself what is on the other side
of what I should be afraid of.

And admittedly, this has led me down a dangerous road
and I have not come out unscathed
but I have come out knowing what I'm made of.
Knowing what I'm willing to be paid for
and knowing what one should truly be afraid of.

And my shadow is not one of those things.
My shadow is me.
I am the light and the dark.
I am a whole being
and I do not deny any part of that truth.

My shadow is my guardian.
For knowing and loving.
Embracing the darkness means that it cannot harm
or scare you because it is you.

So I implore you.
Destroy your shame, call out your own name,
and get to know the parts of yourself
that you have been taught to deny.
And I promise you will live a richer life
if you simply take to heart my unsolicited advice.

## The Ghost Called Solitude
by Martha Flores

The Ghost called solitude is not my enemy.
It is not punishment for forgotten sins or retribution.
It is not a shadow wearing a veil of despair
nor a mask of tragedy bearing a smile or a snare.

## Space Is An Eye Inside Of Whom
by Chad Ruggles

The minds a mess and mine's a mess....

Could you ever harbor truth?
Integrity is the storm pushing each truth to its harbor.

It is the will of God that he should lie?
He created one to do it for him.

Is it for you to decide the difference?

It's a wonderful burden and concern to be able to choose
the identities of those things found to be different.

Things should never be so difficult.
Truth is relative even physical and the thought of itself.

Whoever though decides its dimensions?

Whoever thought the right hand would try to grab itself?

## Language Of One
by Jazmyn Jira

I don't follow a religion; I follow my intuition. I don't go to a church; Earth is my church. I don't listen to a priest but listen deeply to each person that I meet.

God is in both you and me. The only way to find unity is to understand how to communicate beyond what can be written in a script or said in a building keeping us caged in. Words are formed to describe a feeling and language barriers create separation and then judgement due to a misunderstanding.

I believe in a world that knows that no matter what path we follow we all end up in the same whole. If our hearts and minds open to honor the differences of how we each walk we can fill the gap with unconditional love.

Spirit is in constant motion evolving in each breath and there is no way to comprehend it. When we rest our minds and allow silence it all begins to make sense. The beat coming from deep within becomes louder and guides us into a sacred dance.

Stepping into this great unknown sounds can't help but to pour out but this time we don't write them down so that they don't get twisted or keep us from being here now.

Creating in this very moment; a universal language is being spoken. A song that goes on forever with no end, when we all tap in, this world will mend.

## The Human Brain
by Dalila Villamil

The human brain is an organ that has the capacity to receive and emit energy. In this sense, it moves multidimensionally and becomes more complex, as it happens with the universe. Starting from this dynamic, the human brain is a very small copy of the universe. Both designs are governed by mathematical and geometric laws. These laws are those that rule nature, galaxies, and the entire universe. For sure, the great intelligence that designed the universe is a great mathematician! This resemblance between the human brain and the universe is given in structure and energy.

This strictly mathematical order takes place in the growth of the flowers, the human genetic structure, the seasonal cycles, etc. Everything obeys natural and universal laws. Now, if the energy is everywhere, it is logical to think that the information by being energy moves through all the brains and the universe; hence the idea that there is a great universal mind that connects with every human mind. It's like a computer network! Everything points to the fact that the human brain is a smaller scale design of the universe and both revolve around numbers and sacred geometry.

## Sacred Home
by Allyssa Arnold

The Eye beyond deepest darkness, pierced by the Light.

Wholeness, into holy, and then into holes.

Chasing yesterdays and tomorrows.

Unaware of This All; a presence in Now.

This, the Eternal gift, dropping the grasping and aversion
just being in this Here.

You again find your wholesomeness and realize you,
are your sacred Home.

### Anhelos (Original)
by Zoe Zamorano

Quisiera estar sentada ahogada, entre euforia y confort, celebrando lo retórico, riendo con los de antes pero me agobio ante un precipicio de quizás, posibilidades infinitas, verdades absolutas, lenguas, y miradas que maquinan hacia atrás al ver mi rostro.

### Yearnings (Translation)
by Zoe Zamorano

I would like to be sitting drowned, between euphoria and comfort, celebrating the rhetorical, laughing with those from before but I'm overwhelmed in front of a precipice of maybes, infinite possibilities, absolute truths, tongues, and eyes that roll back upon seeing my face.

### Complicated
by Linda Reid

I'm complicated.
You are complicated.
We are all complicated.
With our minds, bodies, and emotions.
With our highs and lows.
With our accumulated baggage from a lifetime of living...
We are all complicated. The world is complicated
and finding our way in it is a maze,
a labyrinth, an untraveled trail.
We are all puzzles with at least a thousand pieces
and we don't get to see the cover of the box
so it is a complex job to make any sense of it.
But when we look up we can find
the Light that makes it possible!

### Roles We Play
by Allyssa Arnold

As I choose to identify less and less with these roles I'm playing, I let go of what should of, could of, would of

been.

I let go of who I am.
I find my most authentic me.
I get to choose again and again each and every moment who I truly want to be.

**Emotions**
by Anabel Watson

We can be anything that we want to be;
that we choose to be.
Why do we let ourselves feel anxious,
because we feel we *should* be anxious,
when we can just chill?

We don't have to feel any which way at all; but we are
pushed around by the emotions floating aimlessly.What
are emotions when all we need in this life is to stay alive.

The rest is up to us, to our emotions, to our selves.


**Untitled**
by Cameron Curtis

Life passes by and now I'm grown.
The time has come to reap what I've sown.
I'm still the same more or less even though
life has beaten me senseless.

Where are the answers?

All the things I thought I would know.
I've jumped through so many hoops
but have so little to show.
I scrape by, my only thought, the will to survive.
Without pain, I'd barely know I was alive,
but what kills me the most is the end of the search
because I won't find what I need in a book or a church.

What use is religion or philosophy in a life consumed
by material responsibility?
But it never ends and I will always search
for answers that were never really there
despite the crushing frustration
that's almost too much to bear.

I'm still a child incapable of self sustaining.
I'm still that nervous teen, trying to cope
with what's constantly changing.
What I build is a series of masks.
One for each moment, encounter, or task.
I move them around, trying to hide my flaws,
but they've drained my life of all purpose or cause.

I hide away afraid of what others might see
but I've completely forgotten which one is honestly me.

## Mixed Bag
by Charles K. Chuckenspire

I'll be damned, if I ain't a mixed bag
and you can write that on my epitaph and laugh or cry.
I'm not gonna tell you what to do with your life.

At first I can come off as indifferent,
piercing, unearthly, glutton for punishment.
Untouchable, effortless, righteously estranged,
gathering sunshine and dancing in the rain;
dancing in the pain.

Dancing the way that someone might dance
when they know that life is made of second chances.

A seasoned fool.
Some might say earned wisdom only comes
from doing things the hard way.

And from wandering galactic backroads
and hearing all that other wanderers have to say.
Becoming a wind-worn cornucopia of stories
and of the many, many, ways that one can find freedom.

Some may call me shepherd, steward, or sage.
I have lived a thousand years
before I showed up on this stage.

If you find me engulfing or surprising
I hope you let that feeling take you
as far as it will go
sucking you in like the undertow.

Others see the pragmatism.
Adaptable animal magnetism.
Efficiency, effectiveness, articulate, deliberate emphasis.
Such a fucking Sagittarius.

Yeah, you got me.

But don't forget the darkness
and the people that I've been.
Sad, scared, weak, and very, very, thin.
Very, very, quiet with almost no will to live.
These words don't come from nowhere
but they're all I have to give.

Inspirational, some say, with tears in their eyes.
Serenity to see through a hardened disguise
because, come on, you guys, you're not fooling anyone.

I know that you're a squishy, searching, love machine,
marooned in a toxic system that circumnavigates
that which makes us human,
that which makes us animals,
that which makes us nature.

For the futures sake,
lean into love and put away your hatred.

And after a few beers, maybe you'll forget about me
but, God, if my words do anything,
I hope they set you free.

And when your oooo turns to oh that's when you'll know
that if I am anything, it's a mixed bag.

# VII

## The Thing
by Jesemynn Cacka

My mind turned soggy like my belly
like the cereal I left on the counter
with good intentions of consuming
but now it's almost dinner
and I've only take two bites
before it turned to paste
like the words on these pages.
Chewed and churned.
Saturated with spit
and intentions of making something better.

But they sit and rot,
under muddy passenger feet,
buried in dirty car floors.
All this time I've spent creating
and projecting the pieces of me in an attempt to make
something whole.

Scattered them across oceans, valleys, and mountains tall
but all the light captured and all the colors imagined
were only cheap substitutes.
A gluten patty overly salted to imitate meat.

A quick fix without the sin but now
I've already done the thing.
Sunk in canines into flesh so deep in a plume of blood
and tearing tendons slapping me in the face.

Satiated.
I did the thing.
I created.
Created.
Created myself whole to wander,
expanded every fiber past it's limitations,
to push a little further.

I've orchestrated my organs to mold another,
I've created life, within the sin of another's flesh.
Some give thanks to God
but mine is the artistry in this creation.

**Kindergarten**
by L. Burton Brender

i was in
kindergarten,
or maybe first
grade, and my
teacher had us
kids pour dry,
colored, detergents
into glass bottles for
our parents.

mine had a little koala
bear on the metal cap. The
teacher helped me pour the
powder in, first the blue and
then the white and then the
blue again.

i took the bottle home
shoved it next to my double
-digit addition, right behind
the lunchbox. when my mom
found out, i remember she
was so proud. i miss her
each time I see it.

### Famous As Fuck
by Mitch McCarrell

When we were kids we all had that someday dream,
making it big on some pro team.
Gayly tapping homers over some big league fence
or maybe ripping rock-n-roll guitars for screaming chicks.
Famous as fuck and surely, whatever the fame,
we'd be kissing busty Hollywood starlets.

But we stopped being kids and many of us seem to be
sleepwalking, strolling while life mocks us,
our hopes on the skids.
Our goals, only wet dreams,
no matter how intense.

Mid-game, we have awoken to find things amiss,
just outside our control,
yet still we are hungry for harlots,
the adulation of the crowd.

In our mind's eye, still lusty, ardent, if a little tarnished,
we're just one scheme short, just one hand up:
Never believing in our souls,
that we could have possibly
pissed it all away.

## Untitled
by Tyler Burlingame

There is a scene viewed here to be had.
Men and Women shuffling in a state of lame.
Driven here, stateless wander;
children no longer lasting in youth.

I am one as if I were with you.

We've gathered and commonly slide astray,
casually it seems,
everyday.

## Sunshine And Rainbows
by Kendra Barahona

Happiness.
Laughter.
Kids running in the water.
Rainbows filling the sky
with happiness.
Smiles on faces.
We're all in peace.
We're all ourselves.
Sunshine and Rainbows.
Putting a smile on our face.

**Picky Eater**
by Kennedy Clark

My palate consists of a thirst for change but a hunger for
repetition.

"I don't like that."
A sentence easily integrated into my vernacular.

For fear of tempting my senses you told me to try but
when I reached for the shelf you told me it was not mine.

Your pitch raising in tune with the fumes streaming from
your ears.

For dinner that night you fed me a main course of scream-
ing, a side of slamming doors, and a dessert of sweet I'm
sorrys'.

When the screaming never seized and your apologies be-
came few,"I don't like that," became cries for the bitter
taste your so called love left in my mouth to be washed
out.

My salty face became fuel to your fire as you scalded my
seven year old ego.


**Fall**
by L. Burton Brender

i'm happy because it's fall.
when the pear leaves drop into a crisp bed under which all
the newborn field mice scurry off to glean the first best
fruits ripened in my orchard.

the morning chill trumpets fresh new season brazenly an-
nouncing there are FESTIVALS AND COUNTRY DANCES
AND DINNERS WITH OLD SCHOOL FRIENDS just around
the corner.

when september explodes i get this giddy thrill just like it's
my birthday or that time when those kid cousins i adored
came back to live next door for a whole month.

i'm so excited i can hardly sit still.
it's there in every passing fairgoer's laugh and in my
neighbor's unwarranted smiles-rushing up on me: that
commanding, untamable, autumn joy.

### Broken Halos
by Sylvia B

Broken halos, fairy dust on the floor,
angles wings cracking...
Neither fly anymore.
Angels not singing anymore.
The trees are wilting.
All you hear is the fairy dust falling
and the halos cracking and the feathers hitting the floor.

Fairy tales were once told
but soon I learned that they are nothing
but bedtime stories and make believe.

My wings have been clipped
and dirt lies here instead of the fairy dust.

All the mermaids have died;
the lagoons have been taken over by plastic.

Once a protecter of nature but now I don't know.

My heart has been replaced.
My hair has been cut.
I cannot frolic any longer.
The fairies stopped flying.
The angles sing no more.
The trees are wilting.
The streams stopped flowing.
The flowers have stopped growing!

All you can hear is the fairy dust sprinkling
all over the floor, "It's just dirt anyways."
The halos are cracking and the feathers are falling,
"It's just feathers from my pillow."
All I feel is the ice freezing over my dying heart.

Everything has gone quiet.
I can't hear the trees whisper.
I can't hear a word from the world where I used to live.

**The Hearts Of Children**
by Pat Turner

Thanksgiving is a time to reflect on what is really impor-
tant. It's not about the food, football, or the mess to clean
up after dinner. It is something more, much more.

I was a teacher for twenty-four years and a substitute for
fourteen. As a substitute teacher I encountered new stu-
dents almost every day. When I was seventeen, a senior in
high school, I was involved in a car accident resulting in
the loss of my right leg. Young children are very curious so
you can imagine the explaining I had to do. The following
examples are what I call snippets from those years.

Sunnyslope, Kindergarten - the day before Thanksgiving
vacation I had a class that was a very social and busy
group. One student in particular was always doing some-
thing; just not what was instructed. After school, the para-
educator took the students outside to meet their parents.
She brought this little girl back to the classroom because
her mother wasn't there to pick her up. She watched me
for a bit, then walked over and asked if it was ok for her to
pray that my leg would get better!

Lincoln Elementary School - While lining up for lunch,
Andres, a Down syndrome boy, made the sign for broken,
while touching my stump. I signed, "Yes broken." He
signed, "Hurt?" I signed, "Yes." He kissed his fingers,
touched my stump, and gave me a big hug.

Sunnyslope, Fifth Grade - When I finished my encourage-
ment talk about challenges and asked if there were any
questions a girl asked, "What was the hardest thing about
losing your leg?" I immediately teared up, took a deep
breath, and said, "Seeing my dad cry." At that time, it had
been over thirty-seven years, but the memory was like yes-
terday.

Lincoln, Third Grade - I had subbed in this class often
during the year. A friend had given me a magazine about
the newest computerized leg in the world of prosthetics.
After reading the article to the class they asked if I was
going to get one. I told them they were very expensive.
How much do you think it costs? They started at ten dol-
lars and I kept saying, "Higher." When they got to five
thousand I told them it cost forty-five thousand dollars
and that was just too much money for me at this time. A
student got up and laid some change on the overhead and
said, "Here's a faith offering!" I WAS OVERWHELMED and
yes cried (oh the faith of a child)! Then everyone got in to it

107

with: "We can bring pennies, one said their Boy Scout troop needed a project, and on it went. Again, OVER-WHELMED, I cried!

As I went through my "school encounter" file, it quickly became apparent the lives I've touched. One student wrote (in her words) a note saying, *"Thank you, Mrs. Turner. I rote this leter for you because you are kind, trustful, and fatful. I pray I will always encounter teachers who have these characteristics."*

I am thankful for having been a teacher and for every encounter I experienced. Thanksgiving really is about something more. For me, it is about the hearts of children.

## Children In Cages
by Martha Flores

Children in cages, excluded, discarded.
Considered the worst of the lower.

Forced abandonment.
By the cruelty of those in power.
Separated from their loved ones.
By the indifference of a system.
Forsaken Children without human rights,
isolated, disconnected by society.
No one listen to your cries.
No one holds you and consoles your sorrow.
In the emptiness of your desolation only memories
and shadows with no tomorrow.

Children in cages; forgotten by the world.
Reduced to worthless.
Children in cages sleeping on the floor.
Abandoned, discarded, treated ruthless.
Without hope, without love, with nothing to look for.


## Bosnia Child
by Gloria Piper Roberson

A child clutches her plastic spoon.
Her stomach an empty milking pail.
Her whimpering echoes from moon to moon.

One ladle of rice, there is more room.
Her eyes beg more than tell.
A child clutches her plastic spoon.

Her cracked lips wilt, tears trickle too soon.
A small plastic bowl of rice to end her hell.
A child clutches her plastic spoon.

Rice lay on her chin in a shadow of gloom
leaving a telltale dinner trail.
Her whimpering echoes from moon to moon.

She seeks a place where sleep will bloom.
Her stomach an empty milking pail.
The child clutches her plastic spoon.
Her whimpering echoes from moon to moon.

## Treasures Of A Grandma's Heart
by Linda Reid

My four-year old grandson wanted to do everything himself, "Self will do it," he proclaimed regularly.

My three-year old granddaughter asked her Mom, "Where did I come from?"

Her Mom said, "Daddy and I made you."

She said, "Did you make me out of play dough?"

Her Mom said, "No, we made you out of love."

My grandchildren say, "Grandpa's favorite color is green." I ask them what Grandma's favorite color is and they both say, without hesitation, "Windigo."

My grandson whispers to me at his father's graveside service, "Mommy has juice in her eyes."


## Cashmere Childhood Brain Dump
by Doug Copenspire

I don't remember most of my childhood. Probably hidden in some repressed memory chamber in my brain. My siblings and I fought a lot. I think it was a way to deal with the stress, as arguments and aggression were what we witnessed the adults do.

One hundred push-ups outside of a Methodist church as punishment for who-knows-what on a fall Sunday morning. Going to bed angry not wanting to fall asleep because I was afraid my anger would be gone when I awoke. A house hoarded, full of magazines and every other kind of excess.

I began to learn what an alcoholic was after moving in with my father. He was my hero...

## Picking Out A Walking Stick
by Rachel Beardslee

I recently found myself walking along an old dirt logging road from my past. As I wandered, the Earth's chapped skin separating under my boots, I rediscovered one of my most cherished memories; walking with my grandpa... He liked to call it exploring... For me, at the age of six, that's exactly what it was.

Today this road doesn't lead to anywhere important but for my younger self, this road lead to every place my imagination could take me. My explorations were dangerous and thrilling and grandpa was always be my side. We were like the modern day Lewis and Clark, The Lone Ranger and Tonto. We were fearless explorers facing danger at every turn.

Before we would embark on our mission we had to gather our equipment. This consisted of one important tool. We had to find our walking sticks. Now, this couldn't be just any plain, old, boring stick. They had to be perfect; comparable to the staff of a king. It had to be sturdy, strong, and tall enough to lean on when we stopped to take a break. After all, it wouldn't be practical to explore hunched over. The perfect stick couldn't be too heavy either. We couldn't allow ourselves to be worn out. It couldn't be bumpy or pokey. We have to be able to grip it comfortably since we would be holding it for awhile.

After we located the walking sticks that were suitable for our endeavors, my grandpa would whittle away all the bumps left behind from small branches that once grew on it. I will always remember the smell. Our sticks were most commonly made from branches; the bittersweet smell was strong and would linger on my hands. The smell mixed perfectly with his already perfect smell. He was a mix of oregano, motor oil, and pine sap.

We would take off on our journey. Where we were going; we wouldn't know until we got there. We were constantly searching for cougars and moose, even though we never did find any, there were so many other things that were fascinating along the way.

The road curves past a pond surrounded by tall grass and cattails, they always seem to be swaying in the breeze. It is the home to frogs, trouts, and turtles. On plenty adventures I'd make it my goal to catch some of the frogs and turtles. With the slippery mud posing a challenge to me my trusty walking stick would come in handy. I would use it to anchor myself as I worked my way towards the edge of the pond. There was an ever-present danger of being dive-bombed by dragon flies, as if they're Kamikaze Pilots

Catching the frogs were a challenge to say the least. They were always hard to see because they blend in so well with the mud and algae around the pond. My stick, once again, became a key tool in locating my next prize. I would poke around the holes made from the cows, whose feet sank in the goo, stopping to get a drink. The frogs liked to congregate there. When I found a crater filled with frog, I would lunge forward into their sticky, slimy, safe haven in hopes of snatching one up. My grandpa would cheer me on; often ready with a Folgers coffee-can to keep them in if I were successful.

On my recent walk, fourteen years later, I was surprised how vivid the memories were. I searched for a walking stick yet again and I took in my surroundings from a different point of view. I listened to the waking aspens shivering in the wind, the frogs croaking, the trout jumping at the bugs that were skimming the surface of the pond, and the familiar buzz of the Kamikaze Flies. I felt the dry, dusty, road that was now hard and compact from years of use. I let the breeze wash over me as my memories brought back the smells I associated with my grandpa. As I found my stick I realized what my stick meant as a child and what it means to me now. It was strong, sturdy, and dependable like my grandfather who never let me down and was always supportive. The stick with bumps represented him and all the things that came from from his being. This time, I didn't cut the bumps away, I held onto them tight; to soak in all that he gave me. The stick was light, like his humor and heart. Now I realize my walking stick represents him and our adventures together. It represents all the joy we shared and who I hope to be someday.

As a child, my grandfather was a playmate and friend to me. As an adult, grandfather is a hero and a role model for all that I was, am, and will be. The memory of him is my walking stick through life, supporting me, guiding me, and helping me through all the exploring I still have left to do.

## The Pit
by Buddy Pierce

There was a place in my hometown of Rock Island, Washington, where we gathered on hot summer days, when we weren't playing baseball. Though we played baseball nearly every day, even youngsters sometimes need a little R&R. On those occasions, we would meet up at "The Pit." It sounds kind of ominous but it was actually just our swimming hole.

First, it was a gravel pit, then, a mile or so downriver from Rock Island, the dam was constructed, blocking the river and raising the water table. Some of that gravel may even have been used in the construction of the dam. Some people, not from Rock Island, or newcomers to our little town may have called it, "The Gravel Pit." We just called it, "The Pit." I doubt if the first letters of each word were actually granted upper case status in how we thought of it but it does make it easier to pick them out of the story.

So, the hole was there, and when the water table rose, it filled with water, deep and cold. Legend has it that people had drowned there, their bodies never to be found. Did they disappear down a hole at the bottom, to pop up in the Columbia River somewhere, eventually becoming food for the giant sturgeon that congregated below the dam? I don't know. Could it be that it was a story, fabricated by Rock Island mothers, in an attempt to keep their children from going there, or at least to be careful? Maybe. Was it effective? Not to my knowledge.

For me, "The Pit" had two purposes: as a place to gather socially and as a fishing hole. At certain times of the year it was stocked with trout. I'm not sure who was behind that; whether it was The Washington Department of Fish and Wildlife or one of the benevolent scions of Rock Island. Suffice to say that as a child, I had wrestled a decent amount of fish from that hole. My brother would take me fishing, out on a point which, if memory serves me (along with a quick check of Google Maps) was at the North end of the pond. But those occasions, though enjoyable, were irregular, and subject to my brother's availability and willingness. I will say that when he was available, he was always willing. Besides being my baseball mentor he also instilled in me a love of fishing.

Far more often, we were there for its primary purpose, as a swimming hole. In those days, it was just one body of water, and most of the gathering and splashing about took place on the Eastern side. That was the only place flat

113

enough and roomy enough for cars to park. The other three sides were higher, steeper, and the water was deeper. We would gather there and laugh and swim and play and sometimes, catch a glimpse of the girls in their swimsuits.

At some point, I don't exactly know when, but more than once, the water level behind the dam was raised. Along with that, the water table, creating more and bigger lakes. The golf course expanded, new houses were built, and the last time I was there, not long ago, my view from the "Rabbit Humps" showed a greener, lusher place than my memory's eye.

## Letter To A Parent Taken By Addiction
by Jazmyn Jira

I have a pain in my heart because I haven't yet met who you truly are. It makes me scream in anger from time to time that what took you away from me is a false world of lies. I know this pain was in you too but you had no idea how to search for the truth. Instead your vulnerability made you a victim to the dead. You killed what you felt and shoved it down to not let it be real. Anything that could numb the symptoms, you took, not realizing you were on the run from yourself. The world told you that to feel is weak but now can you see the mess that has made?

I am thankful for the pain that you gave because it opened me up to my strength. To be strong is not to run but to sit with yourself until the pain becomes just a lesson to keep you carrying on. To feel everything is a blessing because when you finally rise into the light you see that it was the guide. Now I get to look through new eyes, witnessing the beauty, the gift, of being alive. Turn the feeling of pain into bliss. The medicine we give becomes the evidence. It's for all people and can heal any sickness: It's to face the darkness inside that eats away at our life.

One day I pray to meet you in this place and to see you beyond the pain. To watch all the lessons you attained be wisdom for others that are lost on their way. To look into your eyes and see creation unfolding into life. Until then, I will love from a distance and never lose sight of who you truly are. This vision of you I will keep in the heart.

**Children**
by Eric J. Stepper

Letting your kids suffer a little,
it's not cruel, it's educational.

One sweet smile from a child
can erase an ugly morning.

Help your children find their own path.
When it's their own path they will commit to it.

Everybody can be praised for something;
it is currency well spent.

Raising sons is tough but straight forward.
Daughters... They are written in a language all their own.

As parents you are stewards not owners.

Being a parent doesn't come with an expiration date.

When you have children the importance of things changes.

A mother is never finished saying what she has to say.

When raising your children there has to be a balance be-
tween leniency and solitary confinement.

We can be at odds about faith, politics, etc.
but we have common dreams for our children.

When all the kids get a trophy
a sense of entitlement is born.

The best way to parent...?
From your knees.

If you tell your five year old you need their help
and sprinkle a little praise as you pass by,
they will clean the whole house.

Do you want to give your kids a good start in life?
Be interested in them.

You never really know your kids as others do
because if you are in the room
the chemistry changes.

There's no greater sacrifice
than putting your life on hold for a child.

# VIII

### Mornibund (Original)
by Ulises Navarro

Es tiempo.
Solo es mi tiempo.
Solo hoy me pertenece algo.
Solo es, mi tiempo.
Solo hoy puedo sentirme dueño del momento,
el minuto y la ocasión, solo por hoy pude decir que me
adueñe de lo intocable y lo imperceptible.
Hasta el último segundo.

### Moribund (Translation)
by Ulises Navarro

Time.
It is only my time.
Only today does anything belong to me.
It is only, my time.
Only today can I feel I own of the moment,
the minute and the occasion, only today could I say that I
owned the untouchable and the imperceptible.
Until the last second.


### Blood
by Eric W. Fotherby

My Doctor now keeps my blood very thin; he says I must
take my daily Warfarin.

That is where my Spirit hides and resides; it is no longer
like cherry syrup I must confide.

If my blood starts leaking down upon the ground my soul
screams to me a blood-curdling sound.

If my blood won't stop dripping upon the concrete my
hopes and my dreams will end still incomplete.
.
As I feel my life dissipate and beginning to die losing that
vital fluid my heart surely would cry.

I can afford to lose an eye or a limb or an ear but not that
red liquid that my body holds dear!

118

**Reincarnation**
by Anna Marie Sullivan

I have two pictures of my great grandmother
in one she's smiling and jolly,
head turned slightly, rosy cheeked, no filter.

A coy look.
My coy look.
Our eyes break the fourth wall.

In the other she stares stone faced at the camera,
an odd custom of the time.

Uncomfortable.
Stifled.
Forced.
Eyes weary but alert.
I see myself in this too; this cracked mirror.

I wonder which was taken first.

She died the day my grandparents were married.

I look at a picture of her tiny house
and imagine her puttering around near the doorway.

She was forty-two.
I am forty-two.

**Black And White Photo**
by Gloria Piper Roberson

Distant Irish Cousins.
Waterford, Ireland, 1909.

That's golden-haired Cousin Orla, there in the middle,
Cousins Fiona and Sophia after her.

Cousins Hannah and Emma in front; now there
was a true Irish filly.

Emma had rummaged through their nana's hope chest
for those baubles playing off their neck and ears.

For eight years the cousins stashed money like blue jays
to purchase passage to America.

My father told me they were like magnets, living out of
each others pockets, steaming for America on the Titanic
and if blessed, husbands there, for whom they each ached
for like a bunion.

I was eighteen when the survivors came down the
Carpathian ramp in New York.

There was Orla; alone.

She settled in Chicago with us in her own small room
like a cloistered nun in her cell.

Orla spoke only once of the silence from her cousins
in the freezing water and the screaming of the drowning
ship.

My Father told me not to ask questions.

Eventually, she boarded the Great Northern Railway to
Arizona, to live where it was hot and dry, she said away
from water. She died at ninety-four.

She slipped getting into her clubfoot, porcelain bathtub.
Hit the back of her head; drowned.

Never married.

## Scrambled
by Jesemynn Cacka

Crack my skull into a cast iron pan.
Watch a brain sizzle in hot oil, slurry turned solid,
like egg whites with a salty yolk.

They said the weed would do it, leave ya fried on a couch,
melting into fabric like putty warmed by sweaty ass.
No longer forgiving to reshape into nothing
but ground down into weaving patterns
flecked with dog hair.

But it wasn't the flower nor weeks of sleep deprivation.
It was my hormones poured over ice into
a stainless steel shaker, violently jostled
till foam bubbled up, served back to me
in a martini glass, garnished with oysters.

My mind couldn't decode the mixed signals they were
sending, as I took it in one gulp,
shot it to the back of my throat with a cringe
one would make after asking for fifty on seven,
taking the gasoline hose
and shooting it right into the stomach.

Needless to say, I should wear a helmet in the kitchen
and keep my distance from the mixers
poured out from my own mixin's.

These are the reasons that most days
I can no longer read my own handwriting.


## Trapo (Original)
by Ulises Navarro

Las polillas atacaron mi alma, esta llena de ellas,
es un alma vieja y acabada, es un alma destrozada, es
polvo, y del viento esclava, desaparéceme, bórrame, y es-
párceme por otros cielos, deshazte de esta garra sucia y
apolillada.


## Rag (Translation)
by Ulises Navarro

The moths attacked my soul, it's full of them, it's an old
and finished soul, it's a broken soul, it's dust, and a slave
to the wind, vanish me, erase me, and spread me to other
skies, rid yourself of this dirty and moth ridden rag.

## Old Dirt Road
by L. Burton Brender

driving to my father's deathbed
i stop on an old dirt road,

before i look into his strength-robbed eyes
i want desperately to see

this very field that once he, i, and
my brother camped in,

that outdoor morning,
we kids found with wide-eyed delight

a roguing goat bleating his pied piper
summons to crusade,

too young to follow we instead bribed him to stay
with a leftover gum stick fried in an old pan

which in that golden moment between
fragrant mint and being caught

we hurled to the eager siren who ceased
his urging in acceptance of our fellowship offering,

dad—healthy and lean—scolded us only with effort
beneath boyhood eyes.

driving away, i wave farewell to my father
before meeting him spent, and soon to die


## Untitled
by Christine Ingram

Dad was an old dog who crawled to the back of our minds,
died, and stunk up the place.

I get wafts of sorrow now and then, remembering what lit-
tle I can of my father, trimming his whiskers, forgetting my
mum's name.

### La Nada Mundana (Original)
by Zoe Zamorano

Los días siguen sin gloria mueren, persistiendo la con-
tinuidad de los mismos avanzando.

Los días se van, vacíos con los ojos clavados en lo absurdo
perdidos de cualquier dinamismo.

El mundo continúa andando con celebraciones capitalis-
mo, esclavitud, el nobel, los oscares, hambre y guerra, y
yo continúo recordando, observando, asustada, estática,
cobarde, patética, desde mi ventana desde mi nada.

El voyeurismo por la prostitución de la vida de la pereza
de los triunfos insaciables flores, hilos y lentejuelas pasan
con sus secretos y yo aquí sigo, sin poder peinarme.

La gente vive, se nutre, se crea y envenena, se auto
sabotea, y yo solo sigo sin saber trasladarme.

Los enfermos aumentan las reservas para la continuidad
no existen, se extinguen se agotan, y mueren y yo estoy
aquí, llorando hacia dentro soportando el olor a sangre
del pollo rostisado que se come la persona de la mesa de a
lado.

Las horas que me pierdo me estrangulan.

## Mundane Nothingness (Translation)
by Zoe Zamorano

The days continue without glory
they die, persisting their continuity advancing.

The days go, empty their eyes fixed on the absurd
devoid of any dynamism.

The world continues walking with celebrations, capitalism,
slavery, the nobel, the oscars, hunger and war, and I con-
tinue remembering, observing, scared, static, a coward,
pathetic, from my window from my nothingness.

Voyeurism for the prostitution of life, of laziness, of the
insatiable triumphs, flowers, threads and sequins, they go
by with their secrets and here I remain unable to comb my
hair.

The people live, nourishing themselves, creating and poi-
soning themselves, self sabotage, and all I do is remain
without knowing how to move.

The sick increase the rations for continuity; they don't ex-
ist, they run out, they dry out, and die and here I am, cry-
ing on the inside enduring the smell of blood of the roast-
ed chicken that the person at the table next to mine eats.

The hours I lose strangle me.

**Untitled**
by Cameron Curtis

Shadows lengthen and light grows dim
as nightfall comes my thought turn grim.
Though my eyes grow heavy
my sleep will allude me once again.

A shriek!
As a great owl takes flight the field below
trembles with fright.
Tiny creatures scurry obscured
by the darkness behind my sight.

The wind picks up and chills my core.
I know I should retreat indoors but my spirit wills me
to stay and observe this farcical horror.

Rustling leaves raise my hackles.
Are these footsteps on the gravel?
Was that a creaky fence or some maniacal witches cackle?

Soon the footsteps, getting faster,
heralding complete disaster,
walk right up on my heels,
and I cannot contain fervent laughter.

Is there something wrong with my brain?
I'm always at peace with the strange,
has instinct been undone?
Have I got mad or just overly-sane?

Goodnight my diurnal brothers;
you can keep your blissful slumber.
I'll keep to my shadows, for this is my night,
as are all others.

### Plans We Make
by Judie Peavey

One never knows from day to day
exactly what will be.
The plans we make may stand at bay
because of things we did not foresee.

We rise each morn with plans in mind
but some are never born.

For changes are in the air;
we find some for good and some for bad.

Some like a ball of twine unwind
to trip the well thought plans we had
and bring a change of plans to mind.
For some changes we cannot control.

Destiny may change our fate which possibly slows down
our goal and leaves us little to debate.

But true form, one never knows from day to day,
exactly what will be
because the well made plans WE chose
may not be in our destiny.

**The Night Before My Father Died**
by L. Burton Brender

one breath,

two breaths,

an awful pause. And

one breath more;


one breath,

a half sip,

a hollow scream, and

one breath more;


one breath,

a knowing look.

another breath, and

then one more

**Seth, USA Army Special Forces**
by Gloria Piper Roberson

They sent him home from the battlefield to rest
Three weeks to pretend he never saw what he had seen
A time to escape from his death-tortured mind

A time to be with his father and mother
to laugh with his younger brother Ben
They sent him home from the battlefield to rest

He devoured hot dogs with mustard, pizza and burgers
He caught drive-in movies with a girl hot and brazen
A time to escape from his death-tortured mind

He phoned his school pals to chatter
He felt distant; it felt mistaken
They sent him home from the battlefield to rest

He raced his 2000 Harley Davidson up Mt. Hawker
He sped his blue '99 Ford pickup into Backwater Canyon
A time to escape from his death-tortured mind

His uniform in the closet — a hidden deserter
Soon enough he would be back where sorrow is master
They sent him home from the battlefield to rest
A time to escape from his death-tortured mind


**11 A.M.**
by Noah Massey

The unexplainable walkie-talkie echo of the night.
The ghost of a cop on the bridge gives me fright.
The dark illuminated by a single streetlight.
A hundred and eight pennies in exchange for a bite.

128

## Street Of Broken Dreams
by Judie Peavey

There is a street I know where all broken dreams go.
A street where all the pieces fall like puzzle pieces,
large and small.

Sometimes people go there
and try to fit them back together but I have been there
and know the cost because so many pieces just get lost.

When dreams just fall apart
and leave you with a broken heart.
There is a street I know where all the pieces go.


## The Psych Ward In My Head
by Ian Ford

It's not bad yet
but the night train has left the station.
It's only a matter of time till the passengers that
climb aboard along the way will start to make noise.


## A Snapshot From The Shoebox
by Gloria Piper Roberson

I made that quilt for your Great Grandmother Nonni
using Dresden Plate pattern in pink and plum.
She never let it touch the floor, as if an altar cloth,
as if my hands were holy holy.

That is little Samuel tucked in Nonni's lap.
Today, his remains lie tucked
in a grave marked Special Forces, Iraq.
She too fought a battle bravely like Samuel and lost, too,
blown to bits with chemo.

On Nonnie's far right is your Aunt Mary,
then your mother, and then me.
We all had lots of thick, curly, hair back then
except Nonnie.

She shrouded her downy head in white linen
and laid waiting for God to roll her stone away.

## Three Little Words
by Diana Rigelman

What are three of the sweetest words you've ever heard?

"*I love you*," is classic.

Hearing, "*It's a boy*," may put tears in your eyes.

When asked, "*Shall we dance?*" Your heart flutters.

Three little words. So small yet so powerful. Three-little-words changed my life. "*Surgery was a success!*" Followed by, "*You're cancer free.*" Yet what a fight it was to get there...

Darn if that painful spot just wouldn't go away. When I started losing sleep because of pain I began seeking answers. But where to begin in the medical maze of health care?

"I've been a dentist for ten years and found only two oral cancers," declared the Dentist. "And that's not cancer. But you'd need a biopsy to know for sure."

"Where do get a biopsy?" I ask.

"I don't know."

"A bit of steroid cream may fix that right up," said the ENT Doctor.

"I think I need a biopsy, please."

Weeks later when the steroid was of no help he said, "Well, now we'll try a more powerful steroid." Still no biopsy given.

"I don't do biopsies," announced my Family Practice Doctor.

"I don't know what that spot is but it can't be good," claimed my Prosthodontist.

"You need to try miracle mouthwash," said the Oral Surgeon.

"I want a biopsy!" I demand.

"Well now, that's not how this works. You'll have to use the mouthwash first."

It's my life.
It's my fight.

It took seven months of knocking on medical doors to finally get a biopsy for "a spot." I discovered my enemy was squamous cell carcinoma: cancer in my tongue. Shocker. Relatively rare amongst goliaths of cancer, protocol is to excise; cut cancer out. Excuse me? Cut part of my tongue out? How does that work? Images of middle ages torture came to mind. I was told I should expect language dysfunction and prepare for a painful recovery. Would I still be able to talk, enjoy a steak, keep my cowboy whistle? As more questions came; so did the paperwork. Who should I give permission to pull the plug, God forbid, it came to that? Who would make health care decisions should I be unable to make them myself? What will this cost me? I wondered if my will was in order. I realized I couldn't face fighting cancer alone.

After shock and tears subsided, I told a friend. Together we experienced a joint shockwave of horror as cancer news settled in. There were more questions than answers with an abundance of, "I don't knows," I told another my dreadful news. Again there were shared waves of anger, fear, disbelief. It was hard to be honest and open. I hadn't anticipated their feelings of grief and empathy for my journey nor my need to support them. I challenged myself to send out a group private message on Facebook to those far away. In doing so something in my universe changed. Unexpectedly, my grief and fear grew less heavy. Magic started happening as one voice after another told me YES YOU CAN get through this. A healing army began to emerge.

My family rose up. They warmed waiting room seats during surgery. I got an Easter basket of soft toddler food; light hearted provision for post-surgery meals. A friend brought over flash cards of simple phrases to flash others in case I cannot speak and a journal to write that which is unspeakable. Soldiers of support offered errand running, flower watering, bird feeding, bill writing, watch over you and read aloud to you. My healing army grew. A far-off friend offered to travel here to spend the week post-op, manning my meds and the kitchen blender. Friends found empowerment by lending me their strength. We lost the randomness of cancer victimization by sharing moments together.

We're stronger together.
Healing takes time.

131

Words of loving encouragement arrived via phone and computer, text and email. Prayer chains graciously opened their hearts and faith. A heavenly Communication Unit was up and running; believers standing in the gap in prayer to the All-Powerful Creator and Healer. Messages of memories and kind blessings arrived; bolstering encouragement and hope. I wasn't alone in my brokenness anymore. The bond of humanity and compassion brought courage where there was little before.

I learn from my grandson. During a Sunday service he was seated by his mom. Sunshine lit up the small Wenatchee church via stained glass windows. Colored light fell across the pews. When the congregation sang, he started getting squirrely. He began to lift his hands up and over the songbook he shared with his mom so much that she couldn't see the words. His mom whispered, "Sweetie, what are you doing?" With hands cupped upward, illuminated in colored light, he replied, "I'm catching the glory."

Catch the glory.
Believe the best.
Live your life.

**Untitled**
by Ruth Joy

An entirely new thought.

Why do I always feel so odd?
Why do I always feel misunderstood by everyone?
Why does that feeling make me feel like I'm always wrong?
I'm always second guessing myself.
I don't trust a thought in my head.

I blame myself.
Then I don't know if I should
and I find other things or events or people to blame
for my self doubt and indifference.

I want to stop all this sadness and self judgement.
It is sabotaging me and the relationships
I care about most.

I have these quick, abrupt, moments of clarity
when I realize that I am the only me there is
and ever was and ever will be.
That makes me unique in the most beautiful way;
even better than a snowflake.

I am human and I have flaws
and strengths that are all my own.
I am loved for them.
I am precious.

Though I know that all these thoughts are true I can't help
but shake the ones that tear me down
and destroy my inner being.
The ones that want so desperately to be beautiful;
not realizing that I already am.

When I am at my lowest points,
tears uncontrollably running down my face,
my conscious mind always says,
"I just wish someone would tell me I'm beautiful."
Then when the damage is done and the tears are dry,
I realize that that person I crave approval from is myself.

I just wish I could summon
the courage to pat myself on the back.
Just know it's a good thing to tell myself
I'm doing ok for myself.
That I don't always have to be so hard on me.
I am my own worst enemy.

Doesn't that mean I am capable
of being my own best friend though?

I just want to scream out
and let the world know that I'm sort of broken
on the inside.

I just want some help.
But how do I know screaming
and asking for help will do any good.

I'm stranded in the desert that is my own mind.

**Skin**
by Sylvia B

I want to rip at my skin.

THEY SAY, "IT HURTS TO BECOME."

BECOME WHAT I QUESTION! WE ARE ALWAYS BECOM-
ING! WHAT ARE WE BECOMING!

I want to tear this skin off and get some new skin. This
skin I do not like you right now and I am sorry but I can-
not stand you! What are doing! Look at yourself! LOOK!
WHAT IS GOING ON!

Breathe, just breathe, no need to get angry now. Sit down;
breathe. Stop. Go into your head space and be. Be calm
and breathe.

This feeling... It just doesn't want to leave. It hurts so bad
because I just want to fit. Why can't I fit? Why does it feel
like my arms can't hold; please tell what is real. Please tell
me what you see I feel as if I can't. I feel far away. I want
to rip off this body suit of skin. I just do not want it any-
more. I don't want it anymore. I do not like how I feel. This
feeling of not fitting. It is hot and cold and too tight.

Be like a snake and shed your skin.

I AM TRYING! It's just I have to live in this body bag.

It is a process and it takes time; let yourself have time.

It is just so hard and it hurts.

Yes, as it should.

I just don't understand.

None of us understand and maybe that is the point. When
you know, you know. For now, just breathe, just be.

## Blood
by Holly Thorpe

None of the lines in this house look straight.
I'm watching them tilt, drunken,
and thinking of how my skin is so cold
while the blood under its surface is so hot.

I've felt it and been startled by its heat.
Felt some reverence toward it,
watching it fill up a plastic bag
which lay on my arm.
It felt almost like someone else.

I think of the many times
I have not seen the blood on my arm,
only felt it tickling, (raindrops racing
on the windowpane) dripping, off my elbow.

When my skin is cold like cement steps after rain
or kitchen tiles at night,
it feels like something has left me.

Sometimes I hold my veins up to the light
just to make sure they're still there.

Someday I guess they won't be
and that's how I'll know I'm dead.

I'll look as translucent as I feel.

Glow like moonlight,
maybe like floodlights,
like fluorescent bulbs.
Putting out light, yet cold to the touch.

## Wicked Hunt
by Cameron Curtis

There is a beast that dwells within me;
always behind me but never far.
Terrifying, yet, a part of me festering
like some wound that won't scar.
Always hungry and ever formless.

I look back to try to catch a glimpse
yet all my eyes can see is darkness
from the beginning and ever since.
How long have I been running from this?

The monster, with neither shape nor name,
forever seeking its dark harvest.
I cannot win at this twisted game.

No longer know which way I'm running.
I only know that I move away;
is it directing me toward something?

It tells me to move and I obey.
The creature devours all my thoughts,
consumed as quickly as they arrive,
producing only the stench of rot left,
only with that which I despise.

This being has no mouth to speak of
but a void from which no light escapes.

It is the antithesis of love
and truly God's cruelest mistake.


## Desperately Disparate
by Matthew "Suihei" Morgan

I walk a dark and lonely path.
I can barely grasp my past; nothing that lasts.
No coherent thread runs through all I've bled.
Without a steady tone, a person is not their own.
What is the meaning of silence
that cuts you down with violence?
Being lost and aimless is hardly painless,
its cost is truly heinous.
If I am no one, how can I, "Be someone?"

137

## Lost In The Hollows
by Matthew "Suihei" Morgan

Lost in an abyss of supposed bliss;
empty pleasures beyond measure.

How can I not take offense to a world without sense,
when what truly matters
is battered into shattered tatters?


## Carnage
by Anna Marie Sullivan

There are no paintings of the former muse
or peasant girl who amused the king for a time.

Eyes like broken light bulbs,
tears that flow like a river in the dark; not sap.

She's not a tree.

She's a refugee from a war torn heart
that doesn't register her absence;
it just beats on we presume.

London for the short term to recuperate
until the next conquest.

The peasant mucks the muse's stall;
she didn't make it.

Karma from the lady of the manor.

## Robert Stapler's Letter
by Noah Massey

I have an obsession. It's not out of excitement; it's out of fear. It's murder. The news literally gives me a panic attack. I've always wanted to know why someone would take a life, why would someone put a pin in the growth of a grown up baby?

I had to know.

I looked up any modern murderer. Most had died, ironically. Either old age or the electric chair or some kind of needle. I wouldn't give up; my mind needed to rest. Why would you kill? How do you feel afterwards? Where's your heart? Is it still there?

I finally found the name of an inmate from California named Robert Stapler. He had slaughtered eight women, starting in a college campus in 1971, a group of girls in a sleepover in Venice, Los Angeles. It surprised me to read that college aged girls had sleepovers. They were probably getting high or doing something sexual. Maybe they were listening to the Grateful Dead and talking about crushes, who knows? Either way, they all had their throats slit. The next day, a girl in Orange, which coincidentally resides in Orange County, was found dead in a taxi with her throat slit as well. Her fingers were all cut off, maybe to prevent escape, or just for the fun.

Two weeks later, two more girls were found dead in an Indian Wells lake with stab wounds in their stomachs. One man was found as well on the dock, with a suspicious garbage bag around his head and no shoes on.

The last girl (the man doesn't count) was up in Portland, Oregon. She was choked outside of a 7/11, where a smoking teenager saw Robert and ran to a phone booth. Robert probably left California for Oregon because he didn't want people to think he was the same person that shanked the girls in the state below. Unfortunately for his life of crime, the police found the knife in his car and it matched all the previous stab wounds and slashes.

Forty-eight years in an Oregon prison. I did digging and found his location (which I will not disclose) and sent him this letter...

Dear Mr. Stapler...

I appreciate you taking the time to read this letter.

I do hate to bring back bad memories, but I need to put my mind at ease. Why did you do it? Do you not regret it at all? Didn't you feel remorse? They grew from babies just to be stabbed by someone when they're twenty. How could you do that?

I'm sorry if that's intrusive, I just really need to know from someone who has done it.

- Sarah

I dropped it in the postbox and waited four weeks. The idea of his response made me nervous. I could've hurt his feelings; he could've been angry as well. I started hoping he wouldn't respond by week three. He could've been a fixed person now that could've gone without a reminder of why he was incarcerated for life. I felt calmer when I reassured myself I shouldn't feel bad for him whatsoever.

After close to a month of restless waiting, a letter from the penitentiary came. I opened it in my room, waited thirty minutes, then finally gave it a look. It was typed, in contrast to my handwritten one.

Dear Sarah...

I actually appreciated your letter. I love to hear from people I've changed.

I did what I had to do. I had been homeless and cheated on. People wouldn't give my point of view a listen, so I went to great lengths to share my pain.

What ended up happening is that I went to prison and suffered for fifty years. I was a baby too; I was hurt first.

Goodbye.

- Robert Stapler

I read it a million times; analyzed every word. I honestly don't know what any of it means. There are so many different tones he took on. How much of it should I take seriously? I don't feel any better about murder but I know who we should help as a society now. If we keep mistreating everyone who knows what will end up happening? I'm still paranoid and now I can't trust anyone I see on the streets. I don't trust whoever's reading this either. You're probably a slimy judgmental prick of society. Probably in a friend group that loves to pick on other people, right? Stabs each other in the back then gets mad when they find out other people do it too, not taking that as an opportunity to fix yourself? Instead you talk shit about them and become part of your own problem. I'm not religious, but I don't want to go to hell. I know you're all going to be there. I'm not a narcissist but I feel as though I'll be alone in Heaven with all my favorite artists. I'm done writing for you pigs.

Goodbye.

- Sarah

## Words Under Surveillance
by Ian Ford

It's important to refrain from certain hyperbole in a mental
hospital like saying, "bomb" in an airport.

So the best care you get is the care you take with yourself.
Not doing this is the inadvertent choice to become an ani-
mal in the eyes of others.

And since we set ourselves over against nature with roofs
over our heads and paved streets animals are to be feared.

We only like what we can control, that's why we personify
our pets, it's the only way that we and nature have agreed
upon to coexist.


## Addiction
by T.J. Rodriguez

To try again, to die again, I survive the poison's bite.
To try again, to die again, it took but all my might.

To drink from such empty fountains
may make you feel alive but only for a moment,
that part is no lie.

"But this is not a problem; this makes me comfortable
and able to sleep," said Denial's tide.

A wave to which brings sirens,
don't get lost within their eyes,
for I have seen much greater ways
in order for one to cope.

The rising sun on the horizon
brings nothing but true hope.

Yes, now, I finally get it.
Yes, now, I understand.
To try again is to die again and I will be a better man.

**Sweet Sylvia**
by Sylvia B

I want to love and I want the light.

Oh Sylvia.
I feel your blood spilled on the pages full of your poems.

The blood drips with each line you write.
I think there is something living inside of us.

Sleep walking.
Sleep writing.
Not sleeping though
just inside the head.
Entrapped in bed.
Lost in the walls.
Words trying to make sense of feelings?
Trying to get it out just right in just enough time
but there is never enough time
and there is no such thing as just right!

Like a wolf, there is blood in your teeth
but the blood isn't from the catch, it is your own.
Ripping your skin to pieces
because you wish you could rip the world to pieces.

Trying to find change in the world
but keep coming up short.
Playing hide and go seek
by yourself hiding from you demons.

Left alone with your dread.
You tried to cleanse the world of evil
but ended up dead.

The tulips still stand.
The room is still white.

## Midwife Of Death
by Jesemynn Cacka

It was as if I were a midwife of death; the kind to support
a transition but never give two cents worth of my opinion.
I've never died and I don't quite know what it's like, except
for that dream I had of my grinning neck, split wide open
draining the contents of all that I was.

I kept my eyes closed, forced sleep, till life found me again.
Oddly, all there was, was nothing but still darkness as I
ran on E, a taste I wasn't expecting.

I don't think that's how she went out; as we stood bedside
to witness her fitful sleeps and nightmare moaning.

Visitors came and went but I had to sit there never letting
a second pass with empty chatter.

Tears flooded my body as if someone broke the spout off
the piping.

A gush of emotion watching her fragile face twist and pull
in utter confusion in a sleep she never quite woke from.

Me, a midwife of death, holding her hand in support and
in moments of private whispering, kissed her smooth
head, and told her she made it.

To let death come, sweet into the night, to give her true
rest.

I don't know where we go next but she was delivered to
lands of milk and honey, lost love of husbands, and pre-
cious grand babies.

A strained effort of conceiving eighty-nine years in three
nights.

Still, we sat by her bedside with offerings of water, food,
and prayers for an easy transition to long awaited glory.

Dressed in her finest, we kissed her face, told her give it
one last go, as she tipped into where souls flood after over-
filling the cup.

## Farewell Again
by Mike Morgan

I was at work when I got the call. It was from my brother,
Jon. Dad was in the hospital in a coma. Something had
come on suddenly and he was deteriorating quickly. My
presence was requested. I was not prepared for this in any
way. We had just talked a few weeks before and everything
was going OK. Dad and I were never close but we liked
each other and didn't have any outstanding issues. If I
ever had any regret, it was that we didn't spend more time
together. Somewhere between confusion and panic is a
peaceful realm where you choose to feel nothing. That
place is where I chose to go for this event.

I informed my supervisor of the situation and started try-
ing to figure out how to get from Wenatchee to Birming-
ham, today, with no cash or available credit. Riva was able
to get a limit extension on one of her cards and she
booked me a flight out of Seattle. I went home, packed a
bag, got our last few dollars out of the checking account,
and we were off to Seattle.

The conversation on the drive was uncomfortably routine.
We talked about the kids and the beauty of the Washing-
ton landscape and what to do about bills for the next few
days. Anything to avoid talking about Dad. He had been
healthy except for a few minor issues. But seventy had
come and gone and maybe it was just his time. Riva had
already lost her parents and the scenario seemed all too
familiar.

It should have been a routine two hour drive but then the
car decided to audition for a role in the unfolding drama.
We stopped for a burger about halfway and there was
steam coming from under the hood. I am not, never have
been, and never will be a mechanic. After Riva figured out
how to open the hood for me, I was lost. Steam was pour-
ing out from everywhere. I checked the radiator, the oil,
brake fluid, everything I knew to check with my limited
knowledge, and it all looked good, except the steering fluid
was getting low. We got a bottle with our remaining cash
and topped it off.

Now we had to make a choice. We could call a garage,
guaranteeing I would miss my flight, or cross our fingers
and keep going. Missing the flight would leave me with no
way to book another and still in debt for my non-refund-
able ticket. We got back on the freeway. Somewhere along
the way to SeaTac Airport we figured out the power steer-
ing was gone. As long as the car was moving, you could

145

control it. But at low speeds, under ten mph, it was nearly impossible to turn. Getting into a parking space at the airport required backing up and approaching at a dangerously high speed and then banking in at the last second. I'm glad Riva was driving.

The parting was brief. I had to get through security and she had to start calling Seattle relatives to get help with the car. The flight was long. There were plane changes and layovers in Detroit and Atlanta. I had no money for food so over the next ten hours I had two small bags of pretzels and all the water I could drink.

I thought about Dad on the trip. He was a Marine Corps officer and I saw him come and go many times during childhood. One time at an airport, I think when he was leaving for Viet Nam, he told me, "Farewell," and I asked him what that meant. He said, "It's short for *Fare thee well.* Instead of saying goodbye, you're wishing someone a safe trip." I always remembered that and later whenever he got shipped off somewhere I made it a point to say "farewell" instead of goodbye.

Jon picked me up at the airport and we went straight to the hospital. He filled me in on the medical details. Dad had been experiencing breathing difficulties for a few days. They finally went to the emergency room. The initial diagnosis was pneumonia. They wanted to install a ventilator so they could perform more tests. When they did, he lost consciousness, and never came back. After testing the diagnosis was lung cancer. It was aggressive and probably untreatable.

The ICU waiting room was small, just big enough for our family and maybe half a dozen more. It was inhabited for the next four days by me, Mom, my brothers, their kids, and Dad's brother and sisters. Other families and small groups came and went. This room had seen a lot of fear and confusion played out over the years. It was a place for people to wait for bad news, pray for miracles, and evaluate priorities and relationships. Not unlike sitting on the bench across the hall from the principal's office waiting for your parents to arrive.

Fortunately it was payday. There was a cash machine in the lobby and I was rich again! As an added bonus, there was a smoking area right outside from the ICU (imagine that), and a grocery store across the street that sold cigarettes. The hospital also had a 24/7 Subway Sandwich Shop. I consumed a lot of broccoli cheese soup and veggie sandwiches.

146

The next few days were absolute hell. Family members argued constantly, about anything, and everything. Doctors were encouraging us to disconnect life support and limit his suffering. They also mentioned minimizing cost which seriously pissed off Mom. Most of the family wanted to implement any and all heroic measures, holding out for a miracle. I made one emotional plea to let him go but was clearly in the minority. Mom spent most of her time in the room with Dad. She held his hand, stroked his hair, and repeatedly told him what a good man he was. She only went home to sleep. During one of those times I went in to see him alone. I had rehearsed a speech but it all seemed stupid when the time came. I just held his hand and said, "Farewell, again."

The inhabitants of the waiting room represented what remained of Dad's family. Under different circumstances it could have been a nice reunion of sorts but this situation did not bring out the best in any of us.

As the debate raged on about treatment options Mom went home and dug through Dad's files. It turns out that the Marine Corps requires all officers to have a will and Dad had provided one decades before. After weeding through the beneficiary stuff, there were other stipulations outlined. He wanted no artificial life support in the case of serious injury or illness and he specifically mentioned breathing tubes. This was effectively a living will and meant that we were going against his wishes by keeping him alive. After further discussion with doctors, life support was terminated, and he passed within a few short minutes. It was a very surreal if not theatrical scene. The whole family gathered around as the monitors ticked down to zero. I planted my face in my uncle's shoulder for a brief moment and then walked out. This was not a dignified departure and I wanted no part of it.

I was anxious to get back to my family and work and decided not to hang around for the funeral. Before events had a chance to fully sink in, I was on my way back to Seattle. The flight home was rough. This time the changeover was in Minnesota. I had been lucky enough to score a window seat on the Minneapolis to Seattle flight. Then the very large fellow stuck in the middle seat suggested we swap, for obvious reasons, and I complied. The aisle seat was occupied by a foreign lady with a baby in her lap; maybe three months old. I say foreign because she was dressed in a colorful sari that included a head cover; Pakistani perhaps? My attempts to open a dialog led me to the conclusion that she understood no English.

After we were in the air, I ordered the seven dollar and fifty cent "healthy option" lunch, which included salami, cheese, crackers and fruit, and ate it all except for the crackers. The baby started crying somewhere over the Dakotas. The mother rocked and talked and sang even tried a bottle but nothing helped. I wondered what her story was. So young, all alone, in a foreign land, with an infant? Everyone has a story. Everyone has a reason to be where they are right now even if they can't talk about it. There would have been no way for me to describe my last few days to her even if she had known English.

A crying baby gives you two choices; be annoyed or be concerned. I stretched my arms out in front of them. She looked into my face briefly and then handed me the baby. I cuddled it in and looked into the chubby tear filled face. I saw no fear but only discomfort. As a father and grandfather I recognized the look. Instinctively I grabbed a cracker and stuffed it between the furled little lips. The crying stopped instantly and within minutes the baby was asleep. The mother turned sideways, put one arm over the baby, and rested her head on my shoulder. They both slept the entire width of Montana. I did not sleep but rather imagined that I was holding my granddaughter.

After the plane landed and we disembarked she looked at me and expressed her gratitude with a smile and a nod. I answered with a simple, "Farewell."

Riva picked me up at the airport. Somehow she had achieved the necessary car repairs and we headed back to our lives in Wenatchee. Videos of the graveside service were later posted on Facebook. It was very well done. Marines in uniform, 21-Gun Salute, Amazing Grace on the bagpipes. They even managed to arrange overcast and drizzle for the background weather. All very fitting. It would still be a few weeks before the numbness wore off and I could begin the mourning process.

I came home with a new perspective, thanks to a stranger and her baby. Life is what is happening right now. It is not defined by regrets, failures and tragedies, nor by hopes, fears and dreams. Life is happening all around you; right now. Your choice is to let it pass unnoticed or hold it close and cherish it. At some point I will bid my final farewell. But not right now if there are no objections I have to get a load of laundry going, watch a movie with grandkids, and figure out what to do for dinner. Usually, it's really that simple.

### A Portrait Of Courage
by Linda Reid

To me courage is about feeling fearful but taking necessary action in spite of fear. I can think of so many people in my life who have done that but the most inspiring example for me is my cousin Joel. His nearly life-long journey can best be defined by his courageous, optimistic, "can-do" attitude toward the overwhelming obstacles in his life. He was the closest I ever came to having a brother. Our mothers were sisters and our dads were first cousins. I say that made us "double cousins."

He lost both of his legs at the hip due to his injuries in the Vietnam War when he was only twenty-one. His survival was a miracle and his recovery continued through the second half of his life. Almost thirty years after his death I am still inspired by his courage. His life was shortened by his compromised circulation which eventually led to a massive stroke. Even then he struggled to go on living for several more weeks. He died on Memorial Day at the age of forty-two.

Few things ever stopped Joel from doing the things he wanted to do or accomplishing his goals. He almost always found a way over, around, under, or through his obstacles. His wheelchair had "wings" and he kept on "flying" in spite of his physical limitations. He still managed to try skiing, hitchhiking, riding a motorcycle, and driving a tractor on his ten acre farm.

His sacrifice was finally recognized many years after his death in a ceremony in Olympia at the Vietnam Memorial where an inscription memorializes his heroism. His wife, through tireless efforts, made that happen after we discovered it would be impossible to have his name added to the National Memorial in Washington D.C.

His entire nuclear family has passed on now, his Dad, his sister Jan, and finally, at age one hundred, just two years ago, his mom, my beloved Aunt Carol. I am grateful that the blood that ran through his veins will always bind us together as family.

## The Dreamer Dreams Dreaming Dreamers...
by Matthew "Suihei" Morgan

The Dreamer dreams, no loss, no gain,
forever-old, never the same;
all song and game of love and pain.


## Grief
by Katharine Kiendl

Grief is sticky before it dries,
settling on the surface, catching dust and hair.
Warmed it adheres to any solid, dried it begins to crack,
flake, and erode until it becomes dust
blown away by wind.

And while your hand no longer struggles
to separate grief from touch and every part of you
stops being friction against all the adhesion it brings.
When your dust blows way and your surfaces wiped
clean you still find yourself missing what had been.

But grief is also light, ever present with the new day,
hiding in the shadow at night.
Enough to sew seeds on the full moon.
Enough to light the canyon with dappled stars.

It is a necessity.
A knowing of your love.
An exploration of your depth, free diving,
until the pressure becomes too great and releases.
Parts of your heart explode from the tension
only your heart can understand.

It catches you on your shoulder
and tails you like fallen hair,
never enough to weight the user,
only enough to give a sense of disarray.

It reminds you of where you've been,
of who you loved, of why you lost.
But there is no known ending.
No final way to reconcile all the nights you yearn to grieve
for the person as if they only left yesterday.

## Countering Suicide
by Ian Ford

I want to stay alive because of my Pop's hug. It's always a bear hug that lasts longer than most people feel comfortable with.

I want to stay alive because my Mom always wants me to read Kenyon to her and Kenyon talks about her Mother.

I want to stay alive to be with my friends who I know care about me and it's their care that helps me move one step closer.

I want to stay alive so my cat can head-butt my chin because he's discovered he likes my chin close to his face after all.

I want to stay alive to see my roommate have a psychic change because this is the change that matters most.

I want to stay alive for my own psychic change. The change that is infinity and infinity is everyday after I die but also everyday till then.

I want to stay alive in order to become what my psych doctor has hoped I might become.

I want to stay alive so I can meet new people and in return they meet me and together we learn our lessons.

I want to stay alive for black coffee that I drink too much of because the aroma says drink me and like Alice I obey.

There was a moment when I thought all of this wasn't there for my hurt and so I sought to hurt myself but it was me who believed a lie that calls itself distance.

## Moments In Memory
by Ryan Ochoa

There are moments in life I've come to be fond.
It's a tiny lil second when all thought is gone.
It's a fraction of a blink but it seems like forever.
Memories of these moments are my life's little pleasure.

They happen so fast but I wish they would slow.
For a moment like that I just want to hold.
To stay in that time, for second more,
and use that one second more to explore.

The time and the space in between,
what it means to my life, and the purposing.
But that would take away all of the magic.
It's a catch twenty-two and I just can't have it.

Well, cheers to those sweet moments of mine,
giving me goodness I can't even define.
If I died today I would not whine.
For I've collected these moments my whole lifetime.

# IX

**Untitled**
by Betsy Dudash

When Death comes
I will tease, cajole, flirt,
then finally beg.
Cause I, drunk on your love, will insist:
not without my angel.
But Death won't know
that I already won.


**Your Words**
by Martha Flores

Your words fill the empty spaces of my soul.
They feed my mind with loving thoughts and inspiration.
They whisper light in my darkest mood.
Which like gentle music to my ears
become a symphony to all my being.
They caress me, they elevate me, they inspired me.
With the warm touch of your deepest sentiments
your words decorate my soul.
They are the substance of my imagination.


**Untitled**
by Moon Rae

Swallowed by fear in the depths of darkness,
swim to me my darling.
Take my hand, take my heart,
with the moon we will never be apart.

**Broken Wings**
by Betsy Dudash

My words fly free, unfettered, uncaring,
like sparrows on a warm, sunny day.
Till BAM! They hit your heart
like the enchanting reflection.
And lay maimed, confused, hurting,
wondering why.


**Purgatory**
by Anna Marie Sullivan

Dead love if it ever was.
It wasn't a simple overcorrection.

Is cutting his hair without touching him
another hidden grimace?

Saran wrapped dinner plates
go from refrigerator to microwave with ease.

We ate early again; the children were hungry.

The worn sound of his gait and keys.
My nervous system's alarm clock is now theirs too.

Empty gestures, long overdue,
basic decency as a Hail Mary
I fail to Marvel at the heroism.

The impotence forever astounds.


**Untitled**
by Moon Rae

Captured in the webs of your spells;
carried with the winds like a serpent through your soul.
Suffered moments of confusion;
where there's a heart there's a hole.

Becoming slave to the sound of your singing bells.

**Your Light**
by Sabrina B

You are a light my dear.
You are the best kind of light.
The light that doesn't know it's a light,
yet it's brighter than most and you don't know it
because somedays you are caught up
in doubting yourself.

Does it worry you?
Seeing other lights of different colors
shining and dimming?
Do you think you are faulty because you see no color
when you look down at your hands?
You keep your eyes towards the sky
hoping the sun will share her yellows and pinks of the day
and you don't know how brightly you shine.

With every swift movement as you walk
you don't see the majestic world inside of you.
I want to show you what I see because once you get a true
look at who you are there is no turning back.
There is no, "Okay I've seen enough now let's go."
I want to show you the colors
that radiate from your inner core.
They've been there for years but you've never seen them.
Sometimes you mumble about not seeing how your soul
and mine could ever be intertwined.
Darling look at your soul and you'll see
the most fantastic of things.

Your words taste like fruit: fresh and sweet.
It's the way you speak to me.
Allow me to shed my skin.
Let me strip myself of the scarred layers,
the well-known smile, the structure of my body.
Don't look at what is on the outside.

I will tear apart my physical being.
That may sound harmful but you deserve to see my soul.
I transfer the energy in my heart into yours.

Do you feel better about yourself?
There's question in your eyes.
There is no question about it.
You are hot.

When you grab me a sensation I have never felt before
shoots through my body.
When you touch me my soul unlatches itself

from the physical orb it sits in.
My soul is in search for yours whenever I dream.
I may not find you in my dreams
because I find you in what we call reality.

I don't often write about people.
Not about those who have touched my soul before.
You are a muse I never thought I would encounter.
When I kiss you, I kiss you hard,
because my soul is trying to reach out
from under my skin and bones into yours
to create the purest form of affection.
Our souls connecting is a pure form of affection.

On a bad day, when the light inside me is dim
and the walls surrounding me fall, my soul becomes lost.
The colors of your mind find their way to mine.
The world inside of you is not to be feared.

You have galaxies in your eyes.
Permit me to explore them.
I have yet to jump through realities
and I want you to be the first dimension I fly through.

**To The Future**
by Sylvia B

I keep swallowing my heart
or my maybe my heart is swallowing me.
I keep trying to turn it away
but I keep feeling thump, thump, thump.
This heart keeps racing in my chest.
This heart isn't wearing a smile it's wearing a frown.

I'm staring at this door thinking about
how you've been here before.
I'm trying to choke down these tears
cause there's people around.
These tears endlessly flowing.
Endless like my feelings.
Just keep driving.
Just keep crying.
I shouldn't be driving but I just can't stop crying.
There's a hand around my heart and that hand is yours.
I'd give you my heart and my ear.
I just can't stop crying.
This is real and you're not here.
There's a lump in my throat.
I hope you know your hands
are around my heart and on my lungs.
It's hard to breathe.

We are of own destruction,
never wanting to ask one to stay,
never wanting one to sacrifice something for the other,
fear that choosing us over another
was the wrong choice.
So we said nothing...

I'd risk it all for you and you wouldn't let me.
Your words trampled over mine
because you were me and I was you.
You knew what ought to be done...
I wanted you to stay...
I want to stay.
I hope I find you soon.
I hope you find me soon.

## Societal Narrative Of Love
by Anabel Watson

If you love somebody
and you can't do anything about it.
If it's too late.
If it *was* too late.
If it never could have been, is,
and was never cosmically feasible.
If you don't know how to act, how you *will* act,
wondering how to stay sane, when you are,
in reality, in-sane wondering if they feel
the same way about you.
What do you do?
It's too.
True.

At least you know how to recognize.
How to at least try to avoid your own demise.
To feel your feels and let them be.
Free, present, and subtly
Under the surface.
You can't try or even fathom.
You might cry.
But you deny, deny, deny so that you can continue on
and enjoy the life you are lucky to carry along.


## Winds Of Change
by Allyssa Arnold

It's quiet here, the winds have changed,
seasons came and went.
Us...

We remained the same.
The road is coming to a split.
Kiss my lips.
Hold this last picture.
My soul will be close but this body cannot.

You go right.
I'll veer to the left.

Find me someday at our place,
where two worlds become one,
and all is seen clearly.

**Untitled**
by Ruth Joy

How do I make myself special to you?
Perhaps thats not the question I should ask myself.
Perhaps I should ask,"Why does it matter?"
I can't spend the only life I was given chasing you.
Being dragged around in hopes that one day
you'll suddenly realize that I am special to you.

But it seems you're only a boy now.
I simply cannot wait around for you to come around.
I won't wait for you to become a man.
In the time that would take,
I would have become the shell of a woman,
breathing my every breathe just so you would notice me.
This is not the picture of love that I had in my head.
If it was you would actually tell me you love me,
and I would know it was the truth,
I would find myself in perfect harmony with life,
not doubting that even in the worst of times,
I have someone to whom I am precious.

However, my mind sways.

As these thoughts of how I picture you come to me
they go in an entirely different direction.
I start to tell myself, *He told me forever...*
Well... Forever as friends.
But maybe thats all having a life companion is.
Just a true best friend with benefits.
You and I aren't totally co-dependent individuals as it is.
We both have different goals and out looks for our lives.
Maybe we can achieve them separately
but always come back to one another.
I feel like what we have, truly, is a good thing.
I feel like God has intervened in my life and gave me
someone as amazing as you
to open my eyes to beautiful things.
He gave me someone fully supportive of me,
who always says, "I don't ever want you to be
discouraged."

These are the thoughts
on the opposite corners of my mind
that hold the same concerns.
How do I know which to listen to?
I don't want to make any mistakes.
I don't want this to do any more damage
than life has already done to me.
I'm afraid it will turn me into the worst version of myself.

I can see a lonely girl with no confidence;
not one encouraging thought in her head.
She see's only darkness.
She always carries a lump in her throat
and tears behind her eyes.
I see full potential of becoming that girl.
It scares me.

Yet it scares me enough
that I am determined to never know that girl.
That girl will never swallow me up.
She will stay in the darkest corners of my mind.
But as I arise out of this darkness
I am greeted by all of my different decisions.
I try to be so careful not to make the wrong ones
but I'm bound to sooner or later.
It usually happens when I decide to listen to my emotions
(or lack there of) rather than my logical side.

Do I choose to wait and see if you love me
knowing that if you don't I will be pulled deeper
into the darker wells of my being
presented with another challenge
to drag myself out not unscathed?

Or do I leave possibly in the hopes
that you will chase after me for once?
Or do I leave only to forever ponder what could have been?

## Confused pt. 2
by Maximus Ceballos

Hey, it's me, wanna smoke some weed? Help me out and not make me feel like a feign, help me detox, and set me free. But when you leave I feel like a flee attached to the dogs and not to me... I miss the feeling of being free.

I'm sorry for what I did to you. I wish I could be you; so successful and up in the clouds. I'm here trying my best feeling like a clown, the things I say I don't mean, sometimes I say them to just be mean. I don't know why but I just feel like I want to cry, I do my best, but I get so stressed.

I feel like I can't control myself, all I want to do is find some help, I don't want this drought. I love and miss the feelings of your arms when you held me...

**Love**
by Charles K. Chuckenspire

Love fills the cracks in our broken hearts;
it's a pat on the back or handmade art.
It's a gentle sigh made in the dark.
It's asking consent or fanning a spark.

Love can look a lot of ways like a tender gaze
or just texting, "Hey."

Relations shift from friends to rift,
friends again, best friends who kiss.
Back to friends, back to this, back to something label-less.

Our sorrows, our complexity, our yes, our no,
can you just sit next to me?
Can you come over?
I can't stop crying.
Please just listen to my thoughts of dying
and maybe if you can hold them for just a minute
they'll go away and I won't be alone in it.

Love looks like cooking soup with mushrooms.

Love looks like letting go; when you know, you know?

Love is making sure to hydrate first thing in the morning.
Love is paying your bills on time
and telling someone you're sorry.
Love is accepting it when you want to kiss someone
because you think they are just wonderful
and they aren't available or aren't interested in a kiss.
It's being okay with that
and letting your love fill the cracks.
Letting your love look like soup with mushrooms
and space and respect and friendship

When you really love someone it's not about control.

It's about serving that person.
Giving them what you can
because you love giving to them.
Giving them a hand to help them get through this,
not because you want something,
but cause you feel compelled to do it.

Love is all that I am and all that I can offer
and for that I am grateful.

**Sticky**
by Jesemynn Cacka

The constant need to be loved,
turned into constantly touched,
constantly smelled, pawed at.
A basic instinct to ensure survival.

The mixture of sweat; the mixture of scent.
Grimy in hot summer weather; sticky with each other.

Discontent with lonely seconds,
angry at the absence of soft chests,
hearts beating warm, even if we are both
so damn sticky and hot.

There are times I can disappear,
be solo in my existence, as you practice loneliness.
Until you notice I'm gone, then we tango,
back into soft embraces of demanding hunger.

I celebrate the small moments where
I'm un-missed in a hot shower.
I fear our scent will wash down that hungry drain.
I'll be as unrecognizable as a stranger in a crowd.
I fear that your rooting will be dissatisfied
because our skin cells reside where grey waters go
and there is absolutely no way to explain that to someone
who has no context of language.

So before I am summoned.
Before I discover if I'm still your other
or if I've been washed away forever I'll sit on the toilet,
fresh out of the shower, ear finely tuned
for that insatiable hunger, as I chug a cold beer
and piss it out like a grotesque fountain recycling water,
steamy in a bathroom as large as a closet,
resetting my skin to be imprinted again.

The constant need to be loved,
the constant need to be touched,
turned into constant love expressed through touch.

The mixture of us; sticky on one another.

### Vestigio (Original)
by Zoe Zamorano

Tus manos llaman a mi puerta
a la luz tu voz es muda.

¿Por qué abrirte una ventana?
Dejarte pasear por mi casa
cual fantasma permitiendote olfatear mi intimidad
como un susurro que lo registra todo.


### Vestige (Translation)
by Zoe Zamorano

Your hands knock on my door
in the light your voice is mute.

Why open a window for you?

Let you walk through my house
like a ghost allowing you to smell my intimacy
like a whisper that observes everything.


### Good Girl
by Anna Marie Sullivan

I'm not sure if the sudden silence
is what pushes me over the edge or what I plummet into.
Fleeting flashes, awareness, of who I've become,
of what I've allowed.

How little I ask for.
Rightly raised to be so gracious so un-entitled
so content with the scraps.

The others reject; offended.

I was your good girl.
I am your good girl.
You rubbed my belly; told me I was worth it.

I shook my ass and wagged my tail; cocked my head to the
side just so.

Until the wind changed direction and you did with it.

And I wait by the door for my doggy bag.

Such a good girl.

## Raw
by Jana Divis

I woke up that morning just like any other. The repetition of the fan ovulating above my head, the crisp air I breathe creeping into my lungs, the sound of the neglected dog next door barking begging to be let in to escape from the crisp winters end.

As I emerge from the mattress that lies on the floor I smell the smoke you exhale billowing up the stairs and into the hallway knowing that this day is just the same as the day before. I step into the shower and attempt to wash the trepidatious feeling from my skin and every fiber of my being with no hope to be found. I mustered the strength to make myself present to you.

I finally said it, "I'm leaving."

You looked at my with a smug smile; I still hear your words echoing between my ears... "You won't."

Taking another rip from the bong that lay before you. As if time slowed down, I saw you walk out the door. Look at me one last time with those eyes and carry on with your mundane existence. I felt it then. I knew you didn't believe me.

As I packed my things I sobbed to the point of blood letting itself free of my physical form. As I packed the last of my things, you walked in the front door. I felt it then. I knew you knew I was serious now.

As I walked down the stairs I passed the hole in the wall from the night before, my wrists still bruised from your tight grip, that of which you no longer have on me...

**Fishing**
by Holly Thorpe

You fumble for her heart
like some dim light in the dark and seize it.
It squirms in your grip; alive and hot.

You remember stringing worms onto hooks
and how the sun burned, skin blistering, peeling.
The fresh skin underneath like cream: soft and white.

You met her at a bar, never meant to keep her,
although her eyes reminded you of your first girlfriend,
soft and brown and sleepy and that made you feel strong.

You kept her when you realized she was in love with you
and you could make her cry
just by calling her the wrong name.

The first time she said she was leaving,
you laughed at her.
Asked her where she would go at this hour.
She collapsed in the living room.
Slept on the couch.
Pretended over dinner like it never happened.

You haven't fished in a long time
but you remember the feeling of a nibble; a bite.
You know instinctually to move swiftly,
drive the hook deep into the flesh.
Run it through a gill, if necessary.
You know how to hold the line taught.

The day she leaves you beg her not to;
then throw her things on the floor while she packs a bag.
You follow her, screaming, while she quietly removes
her toothbrush from the cup near the sink.
When she pushes past you to put it in her bag,
you break the bathroom mirror.
It will stay broken for months; reflecting you faithfully.

After an hour of nothing, no movement on the line,
you'd pull up the hook, and inspect the pale,
gelatinous thing impaled there.
Picking it off and flicking it into the water,
you'd pluck a red worm from the dark soil,
and begin to twist its thrashing form over the hook.

Watching the sinker carry the line deeper, you swat at
deer flies, that draw blood on the back of your calves.

167

**Touch**
by Kennedy Clark

Touch, sweet touch.
Sensual feelings that don't sit well in the stomach.
Grasping and pushing and pulling and gasping.
A touch that makes my body quiver in agony.
A touch so full of disdain and pain and disgust.
A feeling of being foul.
I want to scream and scrub my body til theres nothing
but bone and raw tendon left; letting the steel wool
rip away at my tainted soul.
No sterilization can fix what has been done.
You can't clean a feeling away.


**Finally Free**
by Kristina Stepper

Young.
Young. Vibrant.
Young. Vibrant and brilliant.
A life to live, so much to give...
And then You entered in.

You.
You. Evil.
You. Evil and cruel
Devil disguised as drink,
Slowly stealing vibrant life
Until her will was won.

Oh, you're good.
There's no question.
Good at tempting,
Good at trapping,
Good at weaving Your web of deceit.

What a waste.
One so young and vibrant
Should have been able
To defeat You.
But it was not to be.
You claimed victory.

Or so you thought...
You see,
Though she is gone
And we're left to grieve,
She's the real victor.
She's finally free.

**Hair Of The Dog**
by C.G. Dahlin

She drank me up and threw me out like the hair of the
dog. Squeezed me dry till I resembled a sullen husk no
longer worthy of passion or touch; left me dirty like bong-
water, laying for the next gunky, junky use.

Words, illustrious flirtatious words, and the cheap heart of
mine. Beauty, hedonistic fallacious/filaceous beauty,
and the threads that so easily forget the pain of the tear.

Maybe it's the danger, maybe its the idea of the stranger,
the one who arrives with the package with your name
slathered all over it. Maybe it's the pheromones and the
allure of a lingering kiss to drive an otherwise still mind to
ripples.

The den drew dark in lieu of such a missing touch, how
these bones forget passion, how they forget disgust,
and how naively the child in us walks straight into a
mossy lake fooled into taking it toward a grassy knoll.

And when life has been so dull, for such an unnoticed
while, one might say, why not ride on the notes of a wile;
to jolt my jugular alive with its jostling choke, maybe to
take in a laugh before the punchline of the joke.

And see, it might seem like a shame, woe is me, heart-
break and love, an ever unwinding trail of users and
abusers and all species of vermin but sad songs are beau-
tiful, and the high that earned them are an irreplaceable
zest to the venerable/vulnerable practitioner; the static
lake got sick of the dull complacency.

And to live, ahh yes, to live, requires throwing an irra-
tional wrench into the clockwork, to knock a few wires
loose to have something new to stitch together; bewildered
and alone again, how refreshing...

With the skin off my teeth, I'm left searching for the hair of
the dog.

## She Quivers
by Diana Rigelman

"Come share your life with me," he said.

She trusted and believed.
He never shared his secret need or that she was deceived.

Their lives intertwined as an aspen grove,
roots deep, productive.
A wondrous trove ever changing
with new generations rooting forth.
Strong, beautiful, re-arranging seasons of life together
until one day he stormed away to live his life different way
leaving her alone.

Dreams and hope were crushed inside.
His lying deception intensified her grieving
as she pondered what part of their life was real.
Could this be how zombies feel; living but not alive?

Her light inside ceased to thrive,
no longer standing tall,
having lost his lub to her dub,
her world felt shamed and small.
While he having shed his bearded night
found his shade of hidden light
growing stronger as he prospered.

The Earth kept spinning as seasons went
before a heart half alive made a valiant ascent.
Believing again, breathing again,
she grew to heal her fatal rent.
Seasons of grief finally spent
when she loved herself again.

Yet, when memories tiptoe through her solitude,
she quivers.


## Ingram
by Sylvia B

Winters bloom; springs goodbye.
A heart growing cold; a heart needing warmth.
Hands must stay open, hearts must keep warm,
never close your lips.
Never let yourself freeze over.
Keep warm my dear.

## Let Love Happen
by Ryan Ochoa

With my eyes, I will look past your imperfections.
With my smile, I will take you far from your depression.
With my ears, I will listen to all you say.

Come here sweet love.
Come here and stay.

With my mind, I'll give you honesty.
With my voice, I'll keep you close to me.
With my lips, I'll touch you tenderly.

Come tangle with me, in harmony.

Let me wrap you with warmth
that only you can feel.
Let me reach for your heart
and ask it to heal.
Let me caress you close as the night unwinds.
Let me be your passion, Valentine.


## The Key To My Heart
by Judie Peavey

Oh, where, my love is the key to my heart?
To tell you, I cannot even start.
It's not in your kiss but more in your hug.
With your arms gently 'round me, my heart feels a tug.

It's not in your words but more in your eyes.
You can speak words of love but they could be false lies.
Your look tells me more than your words ever could.
Your eyes speak more than your lips ever would.

The way that you treat me, the way that you act,
is how I determine your love is a fact.
I'll know by your actions that you truly care.
That you've made my needs your primary affair.

The key to my heart is in your trust.
If you truly love me there can be no mistrust.
And once you have found the key to my heart,
I will never give cause for us to part.

## The Gift
by Sabrina B

I was told I bring out forms of humans that even they
didn't know they had.

"It's a gift and a curse," I told him.

He could only see it as a gift but behind each gift is a mys-
tery no one can explain.

I can bring you back to a time of pain, a memory you
haven't had access to in years, and that scares me.

I will unknowingly cause you to remember the Devil the
first time you looked into their eyes.

There is a part of you, you convinced yourself was a
nightmare, you couldn't bare to wake from. A place where
the darkness was rocking you to sleep only to wake to evil
eyes inside of you. The Devil claws his way into your mind
so you feel as though he became you but, but it's a gift as
well.

I can help you touch the light hidden in your soul. I will
show you how the sun nourishes us and the Earth blesses
us with her beauty.

I can show you the true colors of love: walking barefoot as
the pavement burns your feet or consuming so much air
you feel like a cloud watching over the world as people
who are unaware of their abilities question who they are.

I can help you acknowledge that our existence is only
temporary but that won't stop us from getting lost under
the stars only to find our way home into loving arms.

It's a gift and a curse to allow your genuine forms of hu-
manity seep from your pores.

Your soul has been wandering but I will help you align it.

Yes I can pull away at the black slush inside to make it
feel as though it was never there to begin with. I will put
the energy of the universe inside of you to make you feel
new.

"It's a gift to be able to make people feel the way you make
them feel," he tells me.

Without this energy I am just like them.

My smile isn't contagious; it's the radiation of purity that is contagious.

It's because when I touch you, it's not me touching you, it's my soul and if I have to give a part of my soul to you I will because we are all connected to one another.

When I give you part of me and you give yourself to another we all begin traveling inside each other and that's the gift, a gift from the universe, the gift of energy.

## I Wish
by Charles K. Chuckenspire

I wish I had a passionate lover and an unbreakable heart.
I wish I could rebuild myself
without completely falling apart.

I wish I wasn't so afraid of being alone.

I want to cry, sincerely and fully,
without getting a migraine afterwards.

I wish I liked cats.
I really do; but they make my eyes itch.

I want to be satisfied with a poem
that doesn't go anywhere and doesn't rhyme.
Doesn't inspire anyone, just takes up air, and time.

But I'm a fucking Sagittarius/Capricorn cusp
and everything has to COUNT.
I have to role model perfection, poise, confidence,
and cover up my doubts.
I have to be otherworldly.

I wish I was and I'm glad I'm not.
If I really were otherworldly
I would probably be even more lonely
than the woman who pretends to be strong
and goes home every night alone
and cries and thrashes in the night;
peppering the stars asking questions like,

"Why don't I have a passionate lover
and an unbreakable heart?"

"Why, before I can rebuild myself,
must I completely fall apart?"

Why am I so afraid of being alone?

## Unfolding A Goddess
by Jazmyn Jira

How do you love a Goddess? You take your time. You admire all the beauty she presents but are curious about the mystery underneath. Did she bloom into that flower with pain or with grace?

Before you intake her pollen or eat the fruit learn who is at the root. Ask her about the environment in which she grew, if she had to grow thorns of protection, rise through thick mud, or if she died and had to be replanted.

Doing this will help her grow even more, be brighter, and not fear when people come near her. When asked permission and respected her heart opens to give nectar that overflows the senses.

But to get to her Divine essence, you must start from the beginning and watch her unfold until the end, to the flower that drew you in.


## Unsent Flowers
by Mike Morgan

I sometimes think of the flowers I never sent. I didn't send roses on our last anniversary. I didn't send daffodils when you were feeling blue. I don't get arrangements for the kitchen table, for no reason at all.

I have nothing against flowers. They are a cheap, easy gesture but I usually don't think beyond that. My sin is failing to understand the impact they might have on you. When I am unable or unwilling to show my feelings, perhaps a cheap easy gesture is exactly what is needed.

I am sorry for all of the unsent flowers. They cannot be replaced. But going forward, when I find it difficult to say what I am feeling, I will try to remember the power of a flower that actually gets sent.

## Untitled
by Betsy Dudash

Your voice and your kiss and your touch
awakened me from the nightmare
and bore me in the warmth of your love
to a place of light and peace.
Not a dream, though it could have been,
and if I fall, I know my angel will catch me.


## Our Room
by Linnea Charmaine Rigelman

Sunday sun stumbles in through cracks in the blinds,
across the soothing rise and fall of Marley's freckled skin,
his cool wet nose and lazy soft ears.
The yellowed pages of loved, long forgotten books.
The lackadaisical croon of the radio.
You, absentmindedly rub my feet as you lose yourself
in a stranger's familiar words.
This is the soundtrack of my life.
We are exquisite in our imperfections and I love you.


## Sunset Of Love
by Kendra Barahona

Love is in the air.
Couples holding hands walking down a beach;
an endless beach.
Love is there.
Always there.
Never disappearing.
A stop.
A quick stop.
A Sunset of Love telling us to never give up
on finding the one.

**Fiddler Crab**
by Ray Sharp

Mostly now we act like ghost crabs,
nocturnal, changing color with the tides,
communicating with waves and gestures,
you in harmonious symmetry and I
with my oversized man-claw, monstrous.

When I feed, moving my normal claw
from sand to mouth, it is like I am
bowing a hideous violin, this claw
from Hell, prodigious pincher for fighting
and the bruising old business of love.


**Mantra**
by Michael Reed Schooler

There is no more of your name
I've never heard it spoke
to those I meet who share it
to the *inth* degree
are new to me for they never broke
or made of their love disparate
and I'm not the one that they want to choke

## Moving In
by Sabrina B

You talk in your sleep; did you know? You talk of the man hunting you down or the men you are hunting down. A battle, an adventure, or whatever else is going on behind closed eyes. You often whisper of your undying love for me. My lips curve upward and a grin appears on my face; I kiss you. The smile I held transfers to you as you wrap your arm around me and fall into a deeper sleep. I enjoy watching you sleep.

But while you sleep my mind steps lightly, dancing on the walls and ceiling. I recall past conversations of you asking me to move in with you; a jolt of fear attacks my body. Even though I sleep in your bed every night I latch onto comfort of knowing I have a home away from you. It settles my mind to know I have a quick escape from the world.

Please don't think this is an escape from you. Sometimes dark clouds sit on my shoulders and clouds appear to be light and fluffy but they hold me to the ground and I don't belong on the ground. I am meant to soar above city lights and over mountaintops.

Then... panic sits under my skin as I think about sleeping alone in an empty house, an empty room, but that emptiness shouldn't frighten me when I have lived with the emptiness inside of me for many years.

I hate to say this but you fill the gap and I hate to say it because you can't rely on someone to destroy your inner sorrows or to be the root of your happiness.

You told your friends I live with you but I still refuse to admit that as I hand your Mother green paper someone told us held some sort of value. I give it to her without a second thought but laugh at the idea as I rest my head on your pillows each night.

Maybe fear holds my hand through this because the last time I took this leap of faith a boy put a leash on me like I was a dog that ran away too many times. He tore apart my mind and every thought. My feelings were placed in a glass jar for him to observe as he shook them around. Each belief I tried to understand and explain was incorrect. The mess on the floor was from my lack of discipline, I had no escape plan, there was no map for me to follow.

If I saw him today I'd want to scream, "My drinking problem stemmed from you."

I numbed myself every night; not sure why I was sleeping next to a stranger for a year. I moved five hours away from my best friend, hoping change was all we needed to fix it, but packing up and leaving never fixed what was broken it just left it lying on the ground for him to walk on. He crushed everything he stepped on including me.

When I think about coming home to you every night I hope you don't grow ill from the scent of sweet treats but then again you never liked sweets anyways. You always smile when I arrive but those heavy clouds linger. They slip inside my head telling me you're not like the rest so I should go away for a few days. The voice knows if I go off alone then I will crumble and fall. I don't have a problem being alone but the clouds tell me I'm lonely and I am.

Being away from you for a night shouldn't be this hard. Is it supposed to cause my throat to swell, blocking the air from filling my lungs? My body gets colder each night I'm away from you. I feel myself freezing over without the warmth you provide.

It's not supposed to be this way.

It's not supposed to be like this.

I ache for you.

I crave you.

I know how you hate crowds of people. I sit silent beside you, yet, I feel like the crowd that is surrounding you, bombarding you with questions. I refuse to touch you for fear my essence will overwhelm you.

Kiss me and tell me what I feel isn't wrong.

Kiss me harder and bite my tongue for me because I'm sick of doing it myself.

Kiss me; kiss me and tell me I shouldn't be afraid.

Kiss me harder, tell me I'm okay.

Kiss me.

## So Cracks The Heart
by Diana Rigelman

He couldn't look her in the eye anymore as disquiet in his
spirit grew louder. His nervous knee bounced up and
down in a jackhammer fashion. It didn't take an expert to
read his body language. Clearly he was wrestling with
himself. She knew he'd tell her what was eating him but in
his own time. For now she'd have to wait. Through the
decades she'd learned what was not said between them
was often as powerful as what was spoken. It was an odd
partnership they called marriage; so she waited.

Her thoughts drifted to how they'd fallen for each other as
teenagers. His quiet gentleness and great laugh nourished
her heart. He knew he could do anything he set his mind
to because she believed in him. College years were fol-
lowed with careers, birth of children, buying homes, de-
veloping businesses, and burying their Mothers. Life
twisted with drama, trauma, and opportunity. They'd
started out tadpoles and now were toads transformed
through time by events and choices seasoned with for-
giveness. Their fortieth anniversary dinner was waiting
later in the evening. Her heart beat with gratitude for both
sweet and sour times that brought them to this
day. Through it all they were best friends, still standing.

When he finally spoke she was ambushed by the heat of
his words. His anger seemed to come from nowhere.

She thought it must be a joke when he exploded, "I'm not
going to any anniversary dinner now or ever with you. And
you can't make me."

He smelled of anxiety and rage.

"There was NOTHING, not one good thing being married to
you these forty years. Not. One. Good. Thing."

Confused, she gasped out a nervous laugh.

"Well, the kids and grandkids will be thrilled to learn you
consider them 'nothings'."

Her shield of sarcasm was melting faster than she could
process the emotional explosion before her. Her humor
was failing.

*Wait, what did he just say?*

She couldn't quite grasp his words so much as she felt his fury. Some inner chaos within him was morphing and grappling to find a voice while blasting at her in the process. Could it really be their marriage he was so angry about? No way! Yet, looking at him, she could feel he was in pain. This was no tantrum. Something was deeply wrong.

He backed away from her a few steps as his eye caught sight of something outside. He moved closer to the large picture window eyes fixed beyond what she could see from her chair. As he watched a peace, a tranquility, quickly overtook him. Fiery energy and venomous words stopped nearly as soon as they'd started. He was back in his quiet place stilled by secret thoughts. His signature gentleness was in control. What had he seen that had power to bring his heart ease in his heated moment?

She joined him at the window curious to see what he was seeing. His attention was fixed on a neighbor working in their garden. She felt his emotional shift as his spirit grew calm. As he continued to watch the neighbor she realized his tender gaze was intimate in nature. If a stare could be a visual caress, that was it. That's when it hit her. A fuzzy, life, puzzle piece floating just out of reach, suddenly and clearly clicked into place. In a flash she knew. She knew her husband was in love with the man across the street.

There was an irreparable shift in their universe that day. As shock took over a picture came into her mind. She envisioned two hearts starting to crack. One shattered and burst into pieces, falling lifeless, to the floor. The second heart cracked open too, yet, was transformed. From its cracks deep within it sprouted wings. With a peaceful hope the winged heart flew free.

### Resignación (Original)
by Ulises Navarro

Y me ha llegado la inspiración, esa que tanto se anhela,
pero mis letras solo me atacan y me delatan la maldita
falta de tu esencia y se ríen de mi maldita culpabilidad...

### Resignation (Translation)
by Ulises Navarro

And inspiration has come, that which I so crave, but my
letters only attack me and blame me for the damned lack
of your essence and they laugh at my damned fault...


### You Be A Tree
by T.J. Rodriguez

You're like a tree.
You plant your roots into me
and proceed to grow out for what seems to be an eternity.

I am the dirt and you are the bark and the leaves.
Your essence lands on me when parts of you fall
but your bark stands tall.
I do get jealous of the sun you know;
who you look up to so romantically.
He seems to be shedding his light onto thee;
all while worms are crawling through my bones.

When the sun collapses,
the moon supervises your stillness,
your depression comes with a quickness to bring forth
your memory of me lying beneath you.
I am the dirt and you are the tree...

Thanks for throwing ME a fucking leaf.

As for next time...
Don't.

## Lost And Found
by Ryan Ochoa

Have you ever had a question
which you never learned to ask?
Have you ever felt a random heart
only felt as you two passed?

Have you ever learned to fly
without ever growing wings?
Have you ever lost your hope
then found it where it stings?

I don't have all the answers.
No I won't pretend and lie.
But I tell you, as a random heart,
hope won't ask you to die.

To all the broken hearts, with wings which no longer fly,
cope however you need, because I need you to survive.

But what is hope, stranger?
Just another empty word?
Hope is inspiration when your world turns and burns.

Hope is more than effort.
Hope sings to your heart.
Hope can hide from you too
but you can find it without trying hard.

Hope for all the wishes that your heart can desire.
Hope is not a cowardly thing
for it shines the brightest in dark.

So here's to hopeful moments; hoping you can last.
I hope with every part of me...
Hope and you two crash.

**Relationships**
by Eric J. Stepper

You know you are doing better when she listens to you
and doesn't immediately say, "No."

The duration of a good pity party should be about seven-
teen seconds.

A marriage deepens when you both take the best traits of
each other.

Cradle a person's vulnerability like the fragile, special,
thing that it is.

Love is permissioned discovery.
You let me in; I let you in....
We learn about us.

She influences how I have influence over her.

Relationships are like art; they should provide comfort or
inspiration or both.

Talking is simple; communication is not.

In marriage you start out on different paths.
Love helps you to catch up to each other so you can take
the forks together.

Sometimes the little things like sitting on the couch read-
ing separately but together are big things to your wife.

Promises should be made with a bead of sweat and a drop
of blood.

Prove yourself loveable and worthy every day so that when
you are old and gray, she loves you anyway.

A woman's heart has many rooms.
You need to go room by room and clean out what's there
to put your stuff in.

When your wife comes to you and gives you a big hug and
says, "I love you," remember what you did last.

To really love a person is to know what they need.

**Untitled**
by Vic Tapscott

On the river,
I sit and watch the whorls and whirls
of the past ever flowing to the future.
I wonder as I watch where the past will lead.

For the future is but an uncharted wasteland
full of hidden shoals and unexpected snags.

The past though, the past is to be counted on;
our friend, our confidant, our lover and loved.
Each bit spelled out in intimate detail,
we polish and caress some memories,
obscure and push away others,
but the past is past.

By its very name it is dead and gone.
It is safe.

# X

**The Treehouse**
by Wendy Howard

And it's probably a treehouse...
Cozy and high; hidden.
I let my legs dangle off, sitting naked on sheepskin,
rails, and branches, and incense, and hot coffee
dribbles on my skin.

The cats come to worship me and all that is high.
They offer themselves atop
the most interesting newspapers.
I won't think in terms of practicality,
aging or handicaps, they're already here.
I'll take them by the hand
and climb up to the top and push them off.
They won't feel a thing, till the birds sing, the winds blow,
and I feel like winding my old watch.
Not for the sake of accuracy
but because I like the way it feels between my fingers.

And he's probably a tree man.
Forest through the trees.
If I keep my vision soft, keep my vision fuzzy,
I might see him, dancing.
Not for me but like his life depended on it.

I'll take him to the center,
take him to my bed by the hand,
and we'll climb, where words drop off,
and thoughts fall away.
If love takes root, he'll take wing,
he knows the way home.

By moonlight I dream my baby; hold it in my empty arms.
I am the song of the beloved girl through all time.

It's probably a dream of the tree;
count the rings of my heart.

How many dreams can one heart hold?

**Brilliance**
by Anabel Watson

Delirious. A life trip.
A constant haze: fervently ripping through chaos
in a mad dash toward a calm that isn't there yet.
Deliriously slipping,
up and down on a rollercoaster.
Feeling high. Falling low.
Sooo unknown.
Unknown dynamics where interactions
are shrouded in unspoken truths.
Clouded by our right to fall down
and all around:
Sickness. Weakness. Ness. Ness. Ness.
Like a runny nose, a stomach debilitated
by medicine, by rivers of time eaten up.
By inconsiderate misfortunes unwilling to listen.
By inconsiderate *fortune;* offering a glimpse
of what will never be.
But see...

Where is the breath?

Listen to a truth.
Unperturbed by pleasures.
Engaging where truly felt,
where truly whole.

Listen to a truth.
A timeless expanse.
Fields of it. Flows of it. Freeing by nature.
Follow it and slip it in where possible,
where appreciation is evolve-able
until the haze is a haze no longer
but a balance that evolves into brilliance.

**The Closest Thing To God**
by Kevin Strickland


The closest thing to god that his son ever knew
was the sound of steel-toed boots above
and a thundering kitchen floor.

To anticipate a door, or what's more
the heavy hand that turns it.
And, to still each day at the foot of the staircase
to listen;
for the mumble of private talk,
for the mighty roll of a rhythmic walk,
to fall to all but his knees,
To beg through prayer, "Be the goddess appeased."
To beg through prayer, "Oh god! Just leave.""

Wonder now about the future
be it leather or callous hands?
press the farmers fired iron to flesh
emblazon deep your belt buckles brand
on the back
of the always guilty,
unforgiven,
child of an age old religion

In late days and old man with young mind will remember
his petrified and perilous state,
and will continue to philosophize fate,
as god is
coming down
the stairs.

## Aubade 11/8
by Mitch McCarrell

The rising sun did not disturb my sleep
or dreams because last night I did not dream.
Nor the night before that.
Nor any nights before those that I can recall.

When I was young
I thought the gods spoke to us through dreams.
In my youth I dreamed all the time.
After a dream, all day,
I'd walk around trying to decode
the symbols; to learn the secrets
of what the gods were wanting me to know.

When you get old the gods have forgotten you.
They are busy enticing the young.

I used to dream about my father, him alive,
doing something, saying something.
Always small bits of a life
and for a few days after I'd feel a little happier.

But death is coming and maybe instead of the big sleep
it's a real big dream coming.
Maybe the gods have been saving up really important stuff
and that's when they will return to speak to us.


## The Young Dead Speak Ill of the Old Dead
by Ray Sharp

They complain about the food, lack thereof;
they talk and they talk of the unfairness of afterlife;
how the old dead have their heads in the clouds;
how no one listens anymore, and never did.

The old dead shuffle with their hands
where their pockets used to be, humming
like wind in the pines behind the red barn,
unable to speak since their mouths filled with dust.

**Tetra**
by Anna Marie Sullivan

"We're so little," is what we say once in a blue moon when we stop to marvel at the sky and the scheme of things; at its grandness. Even our words for it all are small and stolen from those who came before and have returned to dust themselves. Are we too preoccupied with our next project or relationship or failure at all of it to do better? Or is it really all too much for our feeble minds to comprehend? Humanity is itself a cliche; a metaphor. The smallest pond of all.

We're fish in a lake. We're bombastic largemouth bass, flamboyant rainbow trout, asshole alligator gar, but mostly millions of tetra swimming for our damn lives. Who has the time or cranial real estate to marvel at the cosmos like the smug hipster fish we revile and envy?

Who can afford the luxury of taking more than a syncopated beat to remember the stars that hang like glowing Barbie Dolls? Why do you think they call them starlets? The moon was an accident like me but the hapless twinkle lights on God's pergola are luminous balls of hydrogen and helium powered by nuclear fusion; whatever that is. The star we call Sun is just the one closest to us. Who would dare to say it twinkles?

Stars are infernos we wish upon, take solace in on lonely nights, wax poetic about to seduce each other, ourselves.

And yet we're made of them; we never forget that part. We're very special supernovas that fell to Earth. Failures for exploding or heroes for daring to take this job and shove it. Just like us.

Tetras, each in our own teacup.

**Mercury**
by Eric W. Fotherby

Phantasmagoric glory riding overhead in the sky to the
deep dark black ebon above. Flying quite high above the
nigh while brightly, colored, streaking, lights are flashing
on by. Ending where I once began my thoughts are taking
me deep into the nether regions of my mind while I travel
upwardly onwards towards the distant galaxies in the sky.

Meanwhile seeking remnants of my original existence and
what would I not give to relive that past but I keep moving
forward. Just like the multitudinous rays of light that are
beaming brightly forward but never to be seen while look-
ing back and only heading upwards into the forever never
and right on up to and through infinity.

This is where my destiny is whispering to me like a faint
hissing sound of gas that always travels too fast as I am
unseen through the looking glass.

While I maintain no past and am now living as a gas and
as it dissipates into the void as the smallest particulates of
matter. So many particles all scattered and as yet nothing
is destroyed. It is only reinvented and redeployed to re-
combine in another place and time, to recreate and to re-
define.

To fill a space and to take up time and then to suddenly
react to this new place and begin a new race. I put on my
game face and I never need to retrace always heading
someplace.

Crossing the universe while supremely hurtling through
space. Sometimes there is a cosmic chase at an accelerat-
ed pace with ephemerals in a gigantic vacuum. Nothing
can be held in place as solar winds are coating the surface
of planets traveling by at a fast pace doing forty thousand
miles an hour while building gravitational power.

For a vapor such as myself I begin from a point and I ex-
pand and enlarge outwardly towards my indefinite length
and with my ability to reshape and to reattach that is my
strength. I can go on to great dimensions and breadths
but I can also swiftly snap back.

I am the ghost from the depths of the bottomless chasm. I
cannot be isolated and I cannot be surrounded and at-
tacked; not even sealed up in glass. I say that only as a
matter of fact. It is not an emboldened act.

For I am an omnipresent being, an all-encompassing gas, my atoms are very loosely attached. I have evolved into a creature that is impossible to grasp not physically nor even mentally.

Now having mutated and transformed myself into a being of an as yet unknown reality, an atomic blast from the past, bits of stardust and ancient matter galacticly discharged into the future. So varied and disparate while racing outwardly towards infinity on photon laser beams.

They are being emitted at light-speed towards my siblings, the Titans, who have been living amongst the stars, and who are all related to one another in this magnificent universe and as yet are so widely dispersed. Very soon their existence is destined to become much more widely manifested and their powers as you will soon see will be so uniquely diverse!

**Dreams Into Darkness**
by Russell Babbitt

Always empty; always left out.

The break of dawn provides more for most than it does for me.

My awareness is constantly dreaming.

Only problem is my avatar has a broken antenna.

I wonder what it's like to remember what stories the group mind has shared with me.

No reason to awaken; not until I get a dream rock to return with.

I can give it to somebody else and tell them it's from the Moon. Nothing lives here; only barren drained batteries.

Half glances occupy my head; others stare intently absorbing every detail.

The squeeze pushes out all that I know and replaces it with handfuls of doubt.

Sand that I thought was surely cement.

Details of nothingness take up no space; at least I'll have room for that Bowflex.

I have three different dreams:

**Good** - in which I can't remember anything but I wake up feeling refreshed and relaxed.
**Bad** - in which I can't remember anything but I wake up feeling anxiety and restlessness.
**Crazy** - in which I remember most everything but it makes so little sense that I struggle to even share it; much less understand it.

Crazy characters melt from friend, to Blob, to enemy.

No constraints of magic and light here, the dream world is all and knows everybody, not saving the good or the bad, simply stirring and seasoning, until the faces recombine and say something unfathomable.

I can't paint my dreams; only blobs of unassuming color dot the page.

**Nothing And Everything**
by Sylvia B

Deafening silence, my ears aren't ringing,
my ears are bleeding.

My eyes are so dry they are shriveling up
and they are about to fall out of the sockets.

I am the radio waves. I am the white noise.
I am projecting it all. I am floating through time zones,
worm holes, and light waves.

I am all the colors that exist
and do not exist to the human eye.

I flew in on a comet and I ate the moon
and swallowed the sun and I choked on space dust.

I am made from the stars.

The ghost of the universe.

I am the extraterrestrial.

Radio waves, white noise, sun beams, moon beams...

This is me.

I am all the moons and the suns and the stars.

I am existing everywhere and no where.

My body is a time capsule and I spinning everywhere.

I am the glitch in the system. The glitch you cannot see.
The glitch that is just a conspiracy.

I've been in a UFO and in the belly of the beast
and I never ate fruit from the forbidden tree.

I have danced with Lucifer and he took my wings.
He took my wings because he gave up his
for the greater good and he wanted to teach me
what it is like to lose something and I do not hate him.

Black silhouettes keep chasing me.

We are playing hide and seek... Or was it tag?

I am existing everywhere;

inside cells, atoms, protons, electrons.

I am not made from them but they are made from me.

God did not make me and neither did the universe;
I was there before the Big Bang.
I saw it happen before it happened
and when it did happen I exploded into a million pieces.

I was then reborn and made anew.

I have seen everything that has already happened and is
about to happen.

Touch me and you will see.

## Polychromatic
by Jana Divis

I've been told my aura radiates
the vibrancy of the borealis;
unable to decode which celestial color
will identify with my soul.

As of late, I'm not sure it has a color at all.
The walls I've built have suffocated the last of the embers
that have fueled my very being.

These walls, made from process, of people,
memories, and dead dreams.

They all coagulate with the cement I pour down my throat
to stop myself from speaking.

It's hardening...
Inching its way up the walls of my ribs,
darkening each cell.

Fragments of it infecting my blood stream.

It's consumed my soul and now I am no longer.

What color is my soul?


## Untitled
by Tyler Burlingame

And now they put this hinge on it.
For it's so dry you need to seal it
and if you don't, it will fade.
So keep it ahold
and wait til it squeezes out of your fingers;
watch it slip away.

Find yourself a smile for it was never yours
and the hours and words you've wasted on this eternal lie
for a while.

And now they put this lock on it.
For it's so great you need to hide it
and if you don't it will fade so keep it ahold
and wait til it squeezes out of your fingers.

So start somewhere, lest you'll ever stop.

**Untitled**
by Adam Leonardini

Three times the movement of the clock
strikes the temple of open eyed fools.

Do not blink, move, or hesitate.
There is blood on the blade.
It does not know sympathy for the bashful.
It moves as if it already knows but does not care the exact
moment.


**05/24/2019**
by Jon Davies

Loquacious, vivacious, enrage us in stages.
The places that save us are cages in cadence
with the beats that bait us.

Afraid? Us?
What's the status of blade cuts?  Mutilate us?
You're in a crazed state, elated to take fake, and debase us
cuz you can't take us past the faded dusk.
That's nightfall, a last call that lasts all of of four hours
to power through without all the alcohol
that pursues suits and turns suites into extensions
of the meet and greets that corporate seeks to delete beefs.


**Insomnia**
by T.J. Rodriguez

If the mind was a pool of water mine would be uneasy.
Sharks break the glass ceiling with a bloodlust crimson
craving, a rippling effect, condemn myself crazy.

If the mind was a pool of water mine would be uneasy.
The moon creates waves, at which all hope is lost, held
high, just to break gravity be the cause.

Lightning storms rage! Thunder disrupts any peace of
sound, all ships sure to sink, men whom die absent of
ground. Rain falls, as have I, frequent detachments from
cloud-nine.

How I feel in anxiety's presence expressed in this
metaphor and rhyme. If the mind was a pool of water, my
ocean be colossally deep, and with so much going on, I
find it hard to fall asleep.

**Everytiiiiiiime**
by Ethan Starkey

At long last.
Uh oh.
Every damn time, get so excited,
my brain can't keep up with my mind.
Ugh, what was I saying?
What were we just talking about?
Ahhhhhh it's at the tip of my tooooongue!
It'll come to me; maybe.
A fully functioning, fully formed, thought forgot.
OH OH OH.
Nope it's gone.

My memory is shot, the short term; the long's good too.
I just don't know why this happens so much.
I got a few thoughts.


**Untitled**
by Ian Ford

I have two brains, one that is peaceful, often catatonic,
the other is a sub four minute mile.
The first allows me to find
the precious hidden treasure of sleep;
while the latter will never rest like a charging bull
that spins in circles.

For over a week now they have been playing catch
and neither holds onto the thought long enough
for me to discern anything useful.
Both of my brains are caught up
in this ongoing volley and I can't keep up.

My eyes darting back and forth
looking inside my head with twitching eyelids.
There's a switch my mind keeps hidden from me
and all of the specialists.
The meds are programmed with instructions
to pin this game down and stand in solidarity
with my peaceful self but for some reason
the perpetrator is illusive;
a mind-fucker of epic proportions.

It appears that my brain is at war with my brain.

## Would You Like To Exchange Words?
by Jon Davies

He asks belatedly, breath baited, legal issues waiting, po-
etry dripping from ripped flesh in his chest beating blood
in bursts of life, swept into dwindling tubes constricting
into capillary single file hemoglobin U-turns.

He asks after hitting send.

He asks before flooding the message exchange with un-
tamed conscious flows growing under tapping thumbs
bumbling in tune to a background hum.

He asks knowing, waiting to share words is the same
thing as wasting away in fear of upsetting the balance of
unrelated weight schemes.


## Restless
by Gavin Johnson

Rest inside my head, is not found easy, but I pretend,
times have found, a place to be, resting inside of me.
With no place to flow, as time will tell, my eyes will drain,
what times are held; glowing in front of me,
I guess I keep wondering.
I close my eyes to see the sea
and si these times push up on me,
Images wash against my skin,
my mind a faucet begins to spin;
my eyes are but the filter, and my lids are but the grates.
Wouldn't it be great, to fix all of these mistakes?
I wash my hands, but never clean them.
I sleep in bed, but never leave them.
When my mind has all but stopped,
I feel as though my world will pop.
If only I could take these thoughts,
put them in a little box,
send them into outer space;
a place to vacuum seal the dates,
big enough to hold our fates.
Far enough in forever's grace,
empty my mind would be;
resting in bed, its' sleep I'd see.

### Bartender
by Jesemynn Cacka

Mister Bartender, pour me up something a little bit stronger. Sprinkle splinters of glass in my dark amber, serve me up a bowl of salted metal nails to ease the hunger, let me chew on the rust to make silver teeth shiver.

Pour the alcohol into cuts I earned diving head first into an empty pool with patches of puddles of leftover rain announcing the coming of winter. I thought the shallow brown would be enough to use discarded cigarette butts as life rafters.

My concussion tells me to heed the no diving signs next time but I hardly ever do anything twice.

Don't misconstrue this for self abuse, I've been stretched to my limit, pushed a little farther, faced my worst anxieties, came through to the other side fully alive with the perplexity to thrive on abrasive sensations.

Mister Bartender, I need that bitter, I need my tongue to shrivel into powder. I need my face to scrunch in twisted form of sour.

Just a lung full of nicotine and a shot of black coffee on shady autumn mornings. Just a night of loud musicians with their mouthfuls of grunge. Teeth black from too many nights howling at cloud covered moons. Blowing my ears out with anthems of ringing I can only hear in the silence, I can barely hear myself think, I do it again and again showing some skin like a butcher's meat case, hoping to bruise in the pit, as easy as a proud man's ego.

Mister Bartender, I like the needles pulverizing my skin with inked out letters beckoning one to pull my hair a little bit harder. Soft touch goes unnoticed, bores me to tears of unchallenged desires. I know I can't smoke in here but I'm going to light it up anyway; file your complaints with Diane and her sentiments will be the same.
Fuck off, fuck you, fuck everybody in this room.

So please, Mister, the man who tends the bar, pour me up something a little bit stronger than that water you got on tap. I crave the brutal sensation of what life's got next, endlessly looping through contradictions of self to keep my toes well pointed. I'm thirsty and I need a rest but I'm wicked and they've got a rule for that.

**The News From Home**
by Mitch McCarrell

First a woman has been fired from the Log Cabin Tav,
shortly before Christmas, so she has posted an ad
selling Christmas presents intended for her kids. A TV, a
Play Station, special controllers. She badmouths her boss-
es; trolls them on a community Facebook page. Her friend,
or maybe soon to be former friend, tells her, "Girlfriend,
cutting down people you know may not be the best way to
live with people in this town."

Weeks earlier there was the dog shot seven times; the
number taking on some special sacredness each time it
repeated. Recriminations flying, threats uttered against
the old man who shot the dog, witnesses ravaged, the
shortcomings of animal control and local law enforcement
outlined in blunt language. Claims by the owners, claims
they would swear to in court, or with their hands placed
firmly on the family Bible; such as the fact that this was
the only time the dog had ever got out. Then the often re-
peated mantra, by the dog's owners and others
who understood their anguish, that, "Dogs are going
to be dogs." This was the absolute logic of which listeners
were expected to understand and honor without
questioning. Then a plaintive defense of the essential
good-hearted lovingness of Pit Bulls and an outraged, "I
am beyond fed up," complaint about people who have sug-
gested otherwise. Finally, the site's arbitrator, closing the
thread, enforcing community peace, reminding users of
the rules. Which several people responded, suggesting the
rules had never been posted, and expressing dismay
over censure of what was only what any sensible person
would know to be the plain truth, and what sensible per-
son could censure that?

I saw an episode of Cops. A show all my people watch and
wouldn't miss. Probably because we might see a friend or
relative being thrown in the back of a cruiser, trussed up
like a holiday turkey. One episode filmed in some small
farming town, the Central Valley, Northern California,
some place frying in the intense cloying heat of summer,
Steinbeck territory, but after he had milked it for any no-
bility it had. Two neighbors, their yards separated only by
a three-foot steel chainlink fence, the battle escalating
with frequent phone calls to the cops, until finally one
neighbor, with a teary voice, calls to say the other neigh-
bor has shot his dog. The camera follows the cops into the
tiny house, through stacks of dirty clothes, magazines,
kids' toys, car parts, back into a bedroom, where the man
who called is down on his knees beside the still form of a

202

pit bull, administering... Administering what...? Mouth - to - snout resuscitation?

God love them and me because I'm one of them. But why in that world, where there never seems to be enough dogs or tattoos, do these lives always sound so much like a soap opera. Not one of the classy ones where people with problems live in some big mansion, set off by a long driveway on a ranch or a beautiful vineyard, and the women wear designer dresses and the men always sport sport coats or suits, day and night, and they hide their worst lies behind lots of money and the only problems the scriptwriters refuse to solve are problems with the hired help.

Now more news from home where the Justice for Poky Campaign is in full swing. Someone with an artistic bent has drawn head shots of Poky on the backs of pizza box lids and nailed them to telephone poles. Someone else on line has asked for a copy of the picture so she can pass it to her son who is a tattoo artist in another town. That way she can have him do a large tattoo (somewhere on her body—so she says) in support of the, "Justice for Poky" campaign. See, how could you make this stuff up? And here's what I hate. While they live in their dog patch dreams of tattooed bliss, they give away any real power they might ever have over their lives, or what happens to them. When the real bad shit descends, someone ends up in jail or dead, they curse the cops and fate, blind fate, but they are the ones who live like blind people, like adult children complaining about unfair parents.

And my post on the community Facebook page was taken down within fifteen minutes: a video showing a woman whose arm was chewed off to the elbow by her pit bull after nine years of a loving relationship between beast and master.

That valley had always been like my Eden but we know what became of Eden. Adam and Eve evicted, later Abel dead and buried, the garden left for those who inherited it by default: Cain and his descendants—oh, and that snake.

## The Python And The Seed
by Faith Merz

The jungle swooned to the setting of the sun as if by some strange force the thick vegetation lit up in shades of orange and gold. Far off in the distance a macaw said its goodbyes to the passing of another day. The clouds that hung low amongst the vines and dreams of green permeated like fractal curtains in the summer heat. The jungle was alive; its moving breath could be felt as the lines of roots and leaves criss crossed amongst the body of earth.

It was here he made home, past the river that churned and swelled, followed by the smallest of paths to the center of a very modest clearing. Tucked out of sight, sat to be, what looked like a hut made out of kindling. Lovingly thrown together, a little window looked out over a very managed and necessary crop as smoke danced from the center of hand thatched straw roof.

This is where our story begins I suppose.

After a day of foraging and trapping, the man of the jungle appeared at the edge of the clearing, ready to appreciate the fruits of his labor. He walked to his dwelling with conviction; a large bundle of firewood perched on his broad shoulders. He wore nothing but a drawstring pouch and a piece of leather made from a giant mushroom tied around his waist. His eyes were striking against his dark tanned skin, great, big, hazel eyes that looked gold in just the right light. His wild black hair stuck out in all directions as it accumulated into tendrils. It was held up by a single strip of leather. Leaves and twigs adorned his head along with his full black beard; a cause he had long since given up on.

It was at this golden hour when he had first heard the noise. Making his way to the river pools as reprieve from the heavy humidity, he waded into the water, letting the cool liquid quench his worn capable body. Floating, the world became silent suddenly, same for the water that gushed around his ears. He heard the faint puttering of his heart as he closed his eyes and felt the muscles in his neck begin to relax one by one. Suddenly it came.

*Dunka/Dunka/Dunka.*

A large sharp sound from the East that made his eyes snap open in bewilderment. Never in all of his years in the wild had he heard such a noise. Firm like a pulse, it caused the water around him to tremor in unison. He waited again noiselessly perplexed by the disturbance. Again it came.

*Dunka/Dunka/Dunka.* A heartbeat in the wild.

He jumped up, forgetting the water completely, he ran to the nearest tree, and began to climb with uncanny precision. Up and up, past the vegetation that hung low to the carbon rich floor, he stopped suddenly as the leaves broke through. From there he perched, straining his eyes for any signs of danger or even worse, man. With their big cranes and heavy metal machines they came constantly followed by great pillars of white smoke forcing him to recede further and further into the depths of the jungle. They always came unannounced, usually over night, to take what they could from a land they did not understand. But as he was perched he saw no malignant machines just the vastness of trees that formed a sea of green and gold. He sat there for a while perplexed by the resonance of its sound. He lay there that night next to the orange glow of his fire and wondered about what was out there that could have possibly made such a noise. As his pondering's ebbed and flowed. The whisperings of the life around him penetrated his mind and soon he found himself fast asleep dreaming of the mysterious heartbeat through the trees.

Many days passed before he heard it again.

He had thought of it many times but had yet to come across its strange pulse again. It was the night who answered for him. Present, in his homely hut, he lay dozing off under the light of a near full moon. He awoke before he even realized he was snapped into space by the vibrations under the Earth. There it came.

*Dunka/Dunka/Dunka.*

He sprang up suddenly, as if possessed, he grabbed his spear and pouch, letting only the moon and the strange heartbeat guide him through the bush. After some time he realized he was running and the pace of the noise quickened to the likeness of a steady drum; his blood rushing through his ears. And suddenly he felt what is must feel like to be a snake careening across the jungle floor or a lemur passing from tree to tree. He felt his heart swell and his muscles extending with the contact of the foliage around him. He felt himself as a wild beating thing running all the while.

Suddenly he stopped. The noise pulsed and swelled to its pinnacle making the trees shiver around him as he

205

stepped into an illuminated clearing. Spear in hand he entered the space slowly; the silver light seemed to play tricks in the dark as his eyes adjusted to the epicenter of the now deafening noise. Before him in the moonlight stood a great Kapok tree and there nestled in its roots, lay a rather small seed, no larger than an avocado. It was bright green; effervescent like the moonlit moss that hung all around the trees. Curiosity propelled him as the noise emanating from the tiny thing shook his bones; the night seemed to hold its breath as he gently picked it up.

Quickly, as if it never happened at all, the noise ceased its beating. Not a sound was made; save the cumulative song of the beasts that dwelled within the night. In a daze he turned from which he had came and made his way back through the thicket, palming, the smooth seedling that pulsed under his fingertips. He wondered about the strange treasure he had found as he made his way back to his hut, stopping periodically to stare at the strange, seemingly ancient carving that was engraved on its hard skin. He puzzled over its origin, growing more and more tired as he watched the now lightening sky turn from black to grey, weariness took a hold of his body like a jungle heat.

Finally he entered his clearing and with the last of his energy he could muster he took the strange seed (somehow compelled) and buried it amongst the vegetation there. With the sounds of jungle all around him, he made his way to his tiny hut, falling asleep as soon as he closed his eyes.

It was deep into the next evening when he suddenly arose, catapulted into reality by the strange events that preceded his slumber. He questioned his memories, bewildered by the small seed, popping his head out of his tiny window only to be convinced of their validity immediately. Before him under the light of the full moon stood a large black shape where he had planted his treasure.

He moved slowly, caution straining his muscles, as if any sudden movements might disturb the foreign thing that waited ominously. He gathered his courage and crept out into the night, coming closer to what appeared to be a huge cocoon, tough with skin like that of a cocoa bean. He marveled at its size, looming over his head it stood over 9 feet tall, he stood there for moment trying reason how such a thing could grow so quickly. Carefully he approached the alien plant and gently placed a hand upon its skin which was surprisingly warm; as if heat radiated from the inside. Slowly, as his curiosity got the best of

206

him, he gave the giant thing a small knock to see if it was hollow. The jungle held its breath as from under the green skin, he felt before he heard, three small raps respond back from within.

He jumped back in surprise, as if he had initiated something, the giant cocoon began to quiver all over. The loud *Dunka/Dunka/Dunka* noise came again. He lay there in shock, mostly powerful fear, as the great thing began to rip itself apart from the inside out. He came to realize, that whatever he had planted was no mere seed, but rather an egg that now was hatching before his very eyes. As this realization dawned upon him a great splitting noise pierced his ears followed by what sounded like the cracking of bones.

To his amazement, there, under the now full moon sprang a woman from her earthly womb. He gazed in awe as she stood there in the night; a look of bewilderment etched into her flawless features. Her skin seemed to reflect the celestial light, darker than midnight, brown and deep like that of the Earth from which she sprang. Her poised limbs exuded grace even through her stillness, raised scars ran along her entire body- ancient, tribal etchings that criss crossed her stoic nakedness. Her black hair cascaded down forming an amalgamation of dread like tendrils that fell past her lower back. Her body was poised and graceful, strong like that of a coiled snake, the muscles of her capable arms flexed as she gained control of her body.

Suddenly out of what seemed like reverence, her head snapped up to the sky, the moon gazed back as if they had known each other for a long time. Her face now illuminated gave light to one of the most ethereal faces he had ever seen. She had full lips, cheekbones that praised the night, a broad nose that had purpose and direction, her face being the only place on her body void of scars. He watched her silently as she dropped to her knees in a kind of silent prayer. Fervently she whispered to herself in a tongue he did not understand. He watched her for some time trying to be as silent as possible until his foot brushed the side of a dry piece of kindling.

Her head snapped up at once. Her eyes met his in the dark. Great peering orbs of reflective gold bore into him like a jungle cat stalking its prey. She stared at him knowingly, unsurprised by his presence, he vaguely registered himself moving closer to those molten eyes in awe. As he did however, the wild woman moved with such agility he barely had time to register it. Somehow through a series of gestures much too fast for him to see she was on top of

207

him, his arms pinned to his sides, he looked up to see her face just inches away from his. A noise quite like a purr could be registered from deep in her chest. Quietly she brought her hand to his face the raised surfaces of her skin sent electricity through his veins. She slowly brought the tip of her index finger to the center of his brow and whispered to all of the jungle with a voice older than time.

"You have known me many times. We have been here before. You know me as I know you. You have found me once again. All the wild beats within you." She released her finger and as she did the heavens opened. A soft starlight fell and his body faded into the soil only to come out as a great python that curled and wrapped around her body. The jungle glistened and sang in unison; a witness to cosmic alignment.

And so that's how the story goes; the wild woman of the jungle whose existence comes throughout time. The python that turns to find her, the wild heartbeat of life, in times of great peril or need, called when the jungle cannot survive alone. He finds her again and again. She gives to that which is broken. There they stay, a perpetual sacred dance, a meeting of two; the python and the seed.

**06/13/2019**
by Jon Davies

Interstellar umbrellar; a cover of cosmic proportions suited to part the particles around you. Astound you and surround you with sounds you compound to nouns to move with verbs you choose to be to. You get to be you, to go see through the torrent of go, be, do. Picking and sticking to what it means to sort and screen the bleed through. It needs you to see to the connections that feed you, breed you, and allow you to achieve that which no one else can dream until you do.

A unique idea to you may be ancient and true, well thought through, and offered like coffee proffered across times lines. An old find from old times, different goal times, rock and roll times, a gold mine of ideas arriving whole and perceived as leaves from family trees across blood lines. Solutions from hard times revised and apprised because they survived for a time as a places mainstay. A hay day before pay got away from foreplay and required a stones bite to light up the night. The days of flint hits and heavy kit that rocks fit into and glass was passed from volcano to humanity in blasts that stashed it from here to Tonasket.

**Cider**
by Gary Trader

Listen up you'anses ta what I'm a tellin ya. Stand becider not in front of er or behinder. Rule and reign together cuz Your Pappy lives inside ya's both.

Cuz theres gonna be a time or two when ya both are gonna have to be in agreement and cum together and you two decider whether a not you are or ya ain't...

Coursin we ought not to be a pushin that envelope on all them women folks else they'll be a tryin to do that decipherin and deciderin on they own.

That ain't too good and right of ya don't be a fussin and a fuedin bout nuttin do it together then when its all said and done you can sit down for a spell and enjoy a nice cup of apple cider with the kin folk this winter...

**"Alex Hayley Wannabe Shtick".**
by Ben Anon

cumm quietly
\indie/     in the back of a Cab.

Hands on the wheel, foot on the brake.
            Lipstick on The Radio.
                        (how would you know?)

Their making up our song
   as we go along,     as we go down
mammary lane, the meter running
            & Cruiseberry lane,    and Snogsbury
Drive            ,

Their taking up our Slack)
            (in the back of a cab, \diptychs/ dipstick
            on the radio, Body fluid Smears
            on the dashboard, Oh yuck Yes.

This is my recurring dream
                        by the way
you're wearing:         champagne & whipp't cream
[ over ] shapeless, spotless slacks.


2 Calling all – slack and Über

to the dance-------floor ...[ no, go another bloc ,
K . U who fantasize
All Fears *. :
You?
            Yes, you there in the back:
keep it in your pants. For now.

**Six Hours Later**
by Chad Ruggles

Try not to think about it.

"Thanks for your service!"

I am hungry.

"Don't think about it!"

Not as hungry as others. (Nobody cares). That makes it easier to NOT THINK ABOUT IT!

You have to buy things twice to keep them once. You bought that tool three times but the sheath you only bought ONCE; that must be why it's gone. Sureeee you liked it...

"It wasn't supposed to be here," I said when the metal detector found it. You put it in the wrong pocket but there it was!

"Yeah, you can't have this in here."

"Right, I know, take care of it."

"Nope."

In the trash it goessss.

I thought, "...It was serving me better."

It's this time around! We throw away treasure! Even people are wasted and squander our resources with pride and arrogance. "The meek shall inherit the Earth." Seabirds hassle eagles 'til they leave.

"...They make more."

Just now thought he didn't have to throw away the sheath too. Didn't even think about it, the guard didn't either, and I guess it's his job to think about it.

I AM WEARY and want this to be over. EVERYBODY STOP FOR A MINUTE!

After the fact, I always learn my lesson: "I should've just left with the knife, hid the knife outside, came back inside, do what I did, go back out, grab hidden knife, walk the same walk HERE, but not knowing any of this."

That's why you got it? Don't mind twice because they always make more and to know value is me insisted upon...
a harder shape and a color more gray.

"But to recover all these things and resolve all this karma will be fun!" That's the idea and I guess it is... I hope it is.

Remember when that thing on the trail, in the dark, in Arkansas Buffalo River Valley, darted away under tall weeds and low hanging trees? Out from under more weeds, dark greens, and leaves growing over the trail reaching to my waist. Then, whatever it was, ran under-or by a nearby tree and there it was in the brush and red light of my headlamp (because it was dark, and so as to NOT ruin my already night vision) breathing in the dark. There was baby pig but alone and quite nice or a big raccoon, not glad to see me. Heavy breathing in the dark, under a tree, late at night, on a trail, in dark-sky starlight northwest Arkansas waterfall country I pulled out that knife... Well, no not that one; that one was lost in Oregon, this one replaced it.

"God that was a bad trip..."

"Why?"

"I was so weak!"

I'm not sure I want to remember how I got so wretched and wrecked; whatever it was, IT paid well. LOST EVERYTHING TO GAIN NOTHING WHEN I LEFT! A surplus lasts less than a month when you give it away.

I like to think, "I'm crazy now," but those things were still being found out!

("Back off, dude! Don't talk about it!")

You insist you're a writer, "It's junk! How many of these have already been thrown away? And by YOU! And other disinterested parties of people!"

Let me tell you about Armageddon: Old men and women don't mind bringing it about but will be dead in a big flowery graveyard and MEMORIALIZED with statues and pictures before it happens.

"I hate that! And I hate you! And I hate them!"

No boy let me tell you about Armageddon: it doesn't have anything to do with a smug Jesus or a hateful fallen angel. Little blonde haired girls will tear their eyes out of their head in front of small, South Carolina churches crying, "I want to see the light!"

And little boys will beat their heads with perfect stone doorstops in discipline to be better. "Now wait a minute, hasn't that already happened?"

"Well... Yeah...."

"And before the wall fell and the whole world was in love?"

"Well, yes, but...."

"And we've had a lot of Christmas and ceasefires and a bunch of little baby angels born since then too?"

"I will tell you one more time before I kill you for good; a mess is a mess whether you are before it, or after it, calling it a mess."

Now, since that is over with, let me tell you about Armageddon. This is it not a thunderous dumb-fuck but a soft whimpering that ends in sleep and a sleep that wakes up to do it all again and again. It dies then is born to begin it again and again. "What about yer folks? How are they doing?"

(THIS IS A HORRIBLE, SUBTLE, MACHINE! THIS HAS TO BE A NIGHTMARE!)

"What were we talking about, boyo? A pocket knife or something?"

**Big Toe**
by Jesemynn Cacka

Grab my big toe; whip me out into space.
Flick my skin reverse.
Instead of tracing patterns moles make
follow the roads in my muscles.

See where I've been
because I'm going nowhere fast without my bones.

A puddle of goo, mashed with an instrument,
intended for ground beef.

I just need a new perspective;
a new vantage on what makes me tick
because old melodies turned screeching in my ears.

Up is down.
Down is up.
Speak in reverse to code tongues make.

There's hidden messages between the lines.
My throat is blocked but brain exploding.
A corked gun backfiring with fragments
of metal embedding in milky white eyes.
Aiming precision.

Grab my big toe; crack me like a whip.
Shake me inside out; I need to hear what is silent and
see what's not there like the hum of space
being filled by vibrations molecules make.

Grab my big toe, whip me back in shape,
fold me like a pretzel, leave me out for five days.
Let the bugs have their munch and mice eat their dinner.
Let them feast on the parts I deemed useless left on the
table with a side of crusty mustard.

I need a new outlook on what it's like to be untouched
hours upon days upon weeks upon months.
Spoiled like curdled milk and overly soft peaches.

Grab my big toe, between thumb and forefinger, and crack
me in reverse; admire the way I look inside out.

## Ode To The Sleepless Night
by C.G. Dahlin

Pretty sure I'm pushing hemorrhoids out my ass.
Tried to kick coffee out of the regiment today,
managed to throw my body into a revolt by 11 p.m.
(Sharp headache.)
I'm talking full head flexing.
Terribly difficult to exist in a body of pain.

So I brewed a cup or two, figured,
"Hey, outta mix it all in the cauldron gut
that's only frothing around two beers,
why not add something to the bare mix."

Substitute the ache for the gurgle and me walking out into
the late night silence to hear a strange squawk
from the neighboring evergreens.

Laying all day to preserve my health.
Wandering all night to make me feel alive.
The windows have frosted over, turned my car's hood into
a fractal of ice, manifesting laniakea over the blue paint
for no eyes other than mine.

Choking down a spliff wondering if I could ever hope to
wrap my head around the sight; the thoughts that churn
from the cauldron gut to the mind eeking through
this night.

The lady told me, "Don't worry the pain will go away,"
and I said, "So will I."

She didn't like that much.
But I have a date with destiny it seems,
brewing up a hemorrhoid in a rich man's ass,
maybe later on, I'll add an extra light to laniakea's
stretching arms.
Maybe I'll end up on a car hood
on a night that nobody breathed.

The revolt has settled;
it now only lives in my darker chambers.
The swelling has gone down, inexplicably,
it's welcomed but without answers.
I can't say what pain awaits tomorrow,
something very familiar, or perhaps a new one.
But for now, I'll remain in the heavy quiet
until the birds start singing
and a new song much like the last,
will begin.

**Untitled**
by Michael Reed Schooler

Your mother really tried to warn you
and the doctor has pills to keep me at bay
but when you catch me, nobody will morn you
and you won't be able to wish me away

I swim in the alcohol that you consume
I am the reason you bark at the moon
I tug at your heartstrings from night until noon
And I will be waiting alone in your tomb

I follow your footsteps, though careful ye trods
and hand below chin, stretched thin with the nods
you know where to find me
at odds with the gods